DYSLEXIA

ACTION PLANS FOR SUCCESSFUL LEARNING

A Practical Guide to Learning Disabilities

Glynis Hannell BA(Hons) MSc

Peytral Publications, Inc.

Dyslexia: Action Plans for Successful Learning
          A Practical Guide to Learning Disabilities   Glynis Hannell BA (Hons) M.Sc

© 2004 Glynis Hannell
10 9 8 7 6 5 4 3 2
Printed and bound in the United States of America

Publisher's Cataloging-in-Publication
(Provided by Quality Books, Inc.)

Hannell, Glynis.
  Dyslexia : action plans for successful learning : a
practical guide to learning disabilities / Glynis
Hannell.
    p. cm.
  Includes bibliographical references.
  LCCN 2003116687
  ISBN 1890455008

  1. Dyslexic children--Education--Handbooks, manuals,
etc. 2. Curriculum planning--Handbooks, manuals, etc.
  3. Special education--Parent participation. I. Title.

  LC4708.H36 2004   371.91'44
                           QB133-1756

Published in the USA
Peytral Publications, Inc.
PO Box 1162
Minnetonka, MN 55345
Toll free: 877-739-8725 (877-Peytral)
Fax: 952-906-9777
www.peytral.com

Index

DYSLEXIA: *Action plans for successful learning*

CHAPTER 1: INTRODUCTION TO DYSLEXIA

CHAPTER 2: READING

CHAPTER: 3 LANGUAGE AND DYSLEXIA

CHAPTER 4: WRITING AND SPELLING

CHAPTER 5: MATHEMATICS

CHAPTER 6: MEMORY

CHAPTER 7: CONCENTRATION

CHAPTER 8: MOTIVATION

CHAPTER 9: PARENTS PROFESSIONALS, AND SUPPORT STAFF

APPENDIX

Chapter 1

INTRODUCTION TO DYSLEXIA

WHAT IS DYSLEXIA?

There is no simple answer to the question "What is dyslexia?" because it is a complex condition that varies widely from one individual to another. All students with dyslexia will experience some difficulties with reading, spelling, writing, and possibly mathematics. Some may have more difficulty with spelling; others may find their greatest challenge in fluent reading or getting their ideas on paper. Each individual is different.

Underachievement is one of the hallmarks of a student with dyslexia. Difficulties in the basic skills of reading, writing, and perhaps mathematics are the almost inevitable consequences of dyslexia. While not all students with learning difficulties have dyslexia, virtually all students with dyslexia will have problems with learning in school. Although underachievement cannot by itself be used to diagnose dyslexia, it is often one of the clearest indicators that the student may have a learning disorder. Underachievement means that a student is not performing to the level that we might reasonably expect when age, ability, and education is taken into consideration.

Students with dyslexia can often be recognized by the level of their responsiveness to intervention. While we can expect all students to respond to appropriate intervention, we know that in comparison to fellow students without dyslexia, students with dyslexia need more intervention for a longer period of time to make the same degree of progress.

Inconsistent performance is another hallmark of the student. Work which the student is able to do quite well one day may seem to be too difficult the next.

The following is a definition of dyslexia as adopted by the Research Committee of the International Dyslexia Association in August 2002:

> Dyslexia is a specific learning disability that is neurobiological in origin. It is characterized by difficulties with accurate and/or fluent word recognition and by poor spelling and decoding abilities. These difficulties typically result from a deficit in the phonological component of language that is often unexpected in relation to other cognitive abilities and the provision of effective classroom instruction. Secondary consequences may include problems in reading comprehension and reduced reading experience that can impede growth of vocabulary and background knowledge.

Dyslexia is also sometimes referred to as a:
Learning disability
Specific learning difficulty
Reading disorder

PREVALENCE

The estimated percentage of students with dyslexia in the United States ranges between four and six percent of the population, depending upon the criteria used and the source. Therefore, statistically there are likely to be between one and three students with dyslexia in any classroom of thirty students. This, of course, will vary from year to year, depending on the distribution of students to each class; some years there may be four, five, or even more students with dyslexia in one class. Because it is such a common condition, it is unusual that a classroom will have no students with dyslexia.

Dyslexia occurs across all ethnic groups and in all socio-economic classes. It also occurs in all languages, although the particular pattern of difficulties tends to vary between languages. It is a lifelong condition, although with appropriate intervention the effects of the difficulty may be reduced over the long term.

Although some people with dyslexia have ongoing, severe problems with literacy for their whole lifespan, many dyslexics proceed to further study, including higher education.

ASSOCIATED CONDITIONS

Dyslexia and Attention Deficit Disorder (ADD) frequently occur together, although the link between the two conditions is not as yet fully understood. Approximately 30% of students with dyslexia have ADD. Low self-confidence, anxiety, and motivational difficulties can be consequences of the difficulties experienced in acquiring basic literacy skills. In some cases behavioral problems may follow.

By chance, the student may also have other difficulties or disabilities that are not in any way connected with dyslexia.

There are other types of specific learning difficulties as well as dyslexia. Students may have more than one type of learning disorder.

Specific arithmetic/mathematical disorder

This is a learning disability in which the student has particular, severe problems in understanding mathematical concepts and/or performing calculations. It can occur independently of dyslexia, but it is often part of the disorder.

Dysgraphia or specific writing disorder

Dysgraphia is a writing difficulty caused by a neurological processing problem (often Developmental Coordination Disorder or Dyspraxia). It is not due to poor muscle strength but is caused by irregularities in the neural pathways that manage the link between brain and hand. A student with dysgraphia finds it difficult to form letters and may have particular problems with sustained writing. For example, the student may be able to write neatly for a few words, but then control deteriorates sharply, and the writing becomes increasingly messy. Although appropriate treatment and practice is helpful, it will not necessarily "cure" the problem.

INTELLECTUALLY GIFTED STUDENTS WITH DYSLEXIA

Intellectually gifted students with dyslexia are an important group with needs which also should be addressed. These youngsters may well be performing within the average range for their age group but significantly underachieving when their intelligence is taken into consideration. The level of frustration for these students is often extremely high, and mediocre literacy skills may easily disguise high intellectual capacities. For teachers, one possible indicator of underachievement is the discrepancy between the student's apparent verbal/intellectual capacities and the student's formal school work. The student who is always quick with an answer or idea in oral sessions but seems to struggle with written language would be a typical student with dyslexia.

CAUSES OF DYSLEXIA

Heredity is recognized as a significant factor in dyslexia, with at least 50% of the students having a first degree relative with dyslexia. Scientists are now beginning to identify the genetic code that is associated with dyslexia.

Dyslexia is a disorder in the processing of information. Reading, written language, and arithmetic involve a complex interaction between listening, language, seeing, remembering, and taking action. Deficits can occur in one or several parts of the circuit required for successful reading and writing. Fluent, accurate reading and writing require the rapid integration of many higher mental functions into one unified, complete process.

Recent studies using brain imaging techniques show that children with dyslexia may process some types of information in a different area of the brain than non-dyslexics. The neural connections that underpin successful learning have may not have formed effectively, so that other areas of the brain, perhaps less well equipped to process the information, have to become involved. This means that a simple task such as sounding out or reading a word may need to be rerouted through alternative pathways, causing a slower and more difficult process with a higher risk of error.

The difficulties a student with dyslexia experiences are not caused by poor teaching, problems with hearing or eyesight, or family tensions (although, of course, these factors can make matters worse).

There is considerable ongoing discussion and debate among experts in the field, about the causes and the characteristics of dyslexia. In recent years, there has been recognition of the central role that phonological awareness plays in dyslexia.

Phonological awareness refers to the ability to recognize sounds within words and to manipulate sounds, for example, blend sounds together in reading or split words into sounds as part of successful spelling. Many students with dyslexia are slow to develop adequate phonological awareness and may experience ongoing difficulties in this area.

A core difficulty for students with dyslexia is in the development of automaticity. They may be able to perform the required skills, but only by putting in a lot of extra effort and working slowly and mechanically. Whereas the student without dyslexia may recognize words quickly and sound out unfamiliar words fluently, the dyslexic student struggles. Words that the student may have seen or written many times before are handled like new words that have to be processed all over again, because they are not yet automatically recalled when needed.

A small percentage of students will have difficulties in the visual memory system. They will have problems remembering sight words, will have difficulties with accurate copying, and will usually be poor proofreaders. Difficulties with the visual recall of printed patterns will lead to a slow acquisition of the link between sounds and written letters at the beginning stages of reading and to a heavy reliance on phonics once the basic letter-sounds relationships have been mastered.

EARLY RECOGNITION AND INTERVENTION

Dyslexia is best managed by early recognition and early intervention. When learning takes place, the brain makes connections which create pathways. As the pathways develop, the brain recognizes previous information when it is encountered again and is able to respond more accurately. We know that young children's brains are resilient. This resiliency allows the brain to make the connections more easily than do older, more mature brains. However, there is never a time when intervention is not appropriate when it is needed. The human brain constantly creates new connections and pathways right through to old age.

The earlier the child is recognized with dyslexia, the more time there is for intervention and the better chance there is of preventing long-term failure and the emotional damage that this can cause. Early intervention also gives the student the best chance of being able to keep pace with peers and prevents the student from falling too far behind. Late intervention often means that there is a lot of catching up to do.

Students with dyslexia often make slow progress in their school work. A lot of effort from teachers, parents, and the student may yield only small gains, and progress may be inconsistent. What the student learns one day is often forgotten the next, so that forward progress is constantly undermined by the loss of earlier learning, which has to be repeated over and over again. This in turn can undermine a student's confidence and motivation. It also means that what is taught needs to be very carefully selected, so that the high level of resources that are needed to achieve success are not wasted on a trivial or irrelevant learning outcome.

Students with dyslexia learn best when they have tasks that build on previous successes and when there is a lot of structure in what they are doing. Students with dyslexia usually need frequent, explicit feedback on how they are doing, so that areas of success or difficulty can be clearly understood.

Intervention is most effective if it is given early and if it is individualized to meet the student's unique pattern of difficulties and strengths. Because learning occurs when connections are made within the brain, it is important that the activities given are specifically targeted to develop the pathways that underpin successful learning. This means that if a student has difficulty in sounding out words, the activities should be developed around the skills required for this task.

This book provides many practical examples of activities that can be used to develop the skills required for successful learning.

DYSLEXIA OVER THE LIFESPAN

Dyslexia is a lifelong condition. However, with appropriate intervention, particularly at the early stages of schooling, many of the difficulties can be substantially improved. The accepted treatment is individualized remedial teaching designed to address the specific difficulties. This is generally combined with a range of compensatory strategies within the classroom.

MYTHS ABOUT DYSLEXIA

Myth
It will click. The child will grow out of it. They all learn at their own rate.

Fact
Students who do not establish adequate proficiency in reading and writing skills in the primary grades are at risk of long term difficulties, unless these students are identified and provided with appropriate remedial assistance.

Early detection makes the treatment of reading difficulties much easier and helps to avoid the loss of confidence and motivation that can easily build up if problems are not recognized promptly. We know there are many early warning signs which tell us which students are at risk of long term learning difficulties.

An intervention program should be commenced as soon as difficulties are detected.

Myth

All students with reading difficulties are dyslexic.

Fact

There are other causes of reading difficulties, such as lack of appropriate teaching, emotional disturbance, general developmental delay, or perhaps a language disorder; these need to be excluded before a remedial program is started.

A comprehensive assessment is essential to establish the cause of the difficulties before an appropriate intervention program can begin.

Myth

The teaching of phonics is old fashioned.

Fact

Recent studies show that phonics instruction is vital in the teaching of reading, especially for those students who have reading difficulties. What other students pick up easily, students with dyslexia may need to be taught step by step, over and over again. Examples may include learning the letters of the alphabet, their sound associations, common spelling patterns, etc.

Many students with dyslexia have difficulties in phonological awareness (the ability to break words down into sounds or to blend sounds into words). Studies show that training in this skill can improve reading.

Myth

All students with dyslexia see print upside down or in reverse, write in mirror image, and are confused about left and right.

Fact

While some students do have difficulty with reversing letters and mirror writing, many do not. Current research indicates that many students have subtle difficulties with language and sounds. Laterality (how the left and right hemispheres of the brain organize information) was once thought to have a direct link to dyslexia. In the light of more recent studies, however, we realize that laterality is extremely complex and that there are many factors yet not fully understood.

Myth

If you have dyslexia, nothing can be done.

Fact

While learning may take a lot of extra hard work, there is much that can be done. First, the dyslexia must be properly diagnosed by a specialist (usually a psychologist or a member of the special education team) who has expertise in the area. Once diagnosed, a teaching program can be tailored to the individual's particular pattern of strengths and weaknesses. Ongoing review and monitoring of progress is important.

Myth
It is damaging to label a child "dyslexic."

Fact
The term "dyslexia" helps to eliminate other common negative labels such as "lazy," "low intelligence," etc., which often leads to a sense of relief for student and parent alike.

Once a student is diagnosed by the special education team, the student will receive special education services under the category of Learning Disabilities. In addition, this diagnosis may also entitle the student to special provisions in the classroom. These provisions are determined by the special education team and documented in the student's Individual Education Plan (IEP). The documented adaptations and modifications may include but are not limited to additional instructional support during class, special testing provisions, modification of daily assignments, and more.

Once the student is diagnosed, parents and teachers can access the extensive body of good quality information, which can lead to significant improvements in the approach used to teach literacy skills.

Myth
If the student were better organized, were better behaved, or had tried harder there would not be a problem.

Fact
We know that some (but by no means all) students with dyslexia do have motivational, confidence, or social problems as part of their learning difficulty. They may have poor social judgment, may be impulsive or badly organized, or may have communication difficulties. This may mean that they do not get on as well as others and that they may think that they are "dumb." A student may try to cover up difficulties by acting like a clown, becoming disruptive, or switching off.

Students may try their best with their school work, only to be told, perhaps time and time again, that they should try harder. Facing constant frustration and failure often leads to loss of motivation and self confidence.

Myth
If the student just practices more, the problem will be solved.

Fact
"More of the same" will not remediate deficits in the complex processes involved in reading and written language. Specific difficulties need direct, planned intervention. Many suggestions can be found within this book to assist in planning an appropriate program.

Myth

Dyslexia means that you will never be able to get a good education or employment.

Fact

Universities, colleges, and schools can all make provision for people with dyslexia to study successfully.

Myth

In the old days everyone was taught to read and spell well.

Fact

There have always been people (often highly talented and famous) who have had difficulties with reading and spelling. Nelson Rockefeller, Thomas Edison, Albert Einstein, and Agatha Christie are all said to have been dyslexic.

Action plans for the successful management of dyslexia

- Given that most classes of 30 children will have about three students with dyslexia, consider screening the entire class for literacy difficulties that have not previously been detected.

- Give all students the opportunity to work in oral, practical, and written modes and then compare the differences in their performance. The student with dyslexia may outperform others in the practical or oral modes but perform poorly in written mode.

- Actively look for intellectually bright students who, although performing at an adequate level, are underachieving. Use both verbal and non-verbal tests, and avoid using tests which require high-level reading or writing skills.

- Parents are often the ones who see a very bright youngster at home becoming a "dumb" student at school. Check with parents of all students about whether they feel their child is performing up to their expectations.

- Given that dyslexia is often an inherited condition, ask parents to indicate whether there is a family history of dyslexia (in any situation where there is concern about a student's progress or performance.)

- View students with poor literacy skills (untidy writing, inaccurate copying, poor spelling, reluctance to read) as possible students with dyslexia rather than students of limited ability

- View students with behavioral problems who have become discouraged and negative because of learning difficulties as possible students with dyslexia.

- View students who are extremely disorganized as possibly having dyslexia (with or without Attention Deficit Disorder).

- Value oral and practical work, and make sure that all students have the opportunity to demonstrate their skills in tasks which are free of literacy requirements.

- Ensure that all students with dyslexia have appropriate remedial assistance (see later chapters of this book).

- Ensure that all students with dyslexia have appropriate adjustments and accommodations to allow them to access the curriculum (see later sections of this book).

- Ensure that all students with dyslexia have appropriate modifications and accommodations when they are being assessed (see later sections of this book).

- Keep informed of current developments in the understanding of dyslexia by joining appropriate organizations, reading professional journals and information sources, and attending conferences.

- You will find a wide range of suggestions contained in the following pages of this book; please refer to them to develop action plans for successful learning for your students.

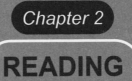

Chapter 2

READING

READING, DYSLEXIA, AND SCHOOLWORK

Reading difficulties are among the most obvious signs of dyslexia. While a student may eventually acquire basic reading skills the process is much slower and needs much more teacher and parent input than would normally be expected.

Reading is a complex process. At the beginning stages the student has to recognize individual letters and remember their sounds. These sounds have to be blended into whole words, and the whole words have to be understood as part of a sentence. The students draw on their underlying knowledge of language structures to anticipate the next word in a sentence and to understand what has been read. In the English language the student also has to recognize some words as irregular and know these words by sight.

A young student with dyslexia may be very slow to pick up the basics of letters and their sounds, and may have great difficulty in blending the sounds together to make a word.

> John, now a very successful business man, remembered his early years at school:
>
> I used to look at the other kids. They just knew those words. I used to think to myself, 'How do they do that?' I'd pick up the book at look at all those letters-they just didn't make any sense to me-just black letters all over the page. My mother and my teachers worked and worked with me, and sometimes I could just sense their frustration. I had one teacher who used to tap her pencil while she waited for me to read the next word- guess she hated my reading session as much as I did!

Students with dyslexia find it difficult to remember the appearance of words that they may have seen many times before. This means they have to stop and sound out the word or guess by using context over and over again.

Bright students may have good reading comprehension but poor accuracy.

When students have reading difficulties, they will have problems with many aspects of their school work. They may not be able to read well enough to understand worksheets (even though they could do the tasks easily if they could read what to do). Their reading may be painfully slow. Researching for a project will be a challenge. Limited reading skills make locating appropriate reference material very difficult indeed. Difficulties in reading a test may damage the students' chances of demonstrating their knowledge of a topic.

Well, you see you have to sit there and look like you are reading, so I count letters...its really good...your eyes move just like you are reading...mostly I do the alphabet...and the first page I count how many "a's" I can see, then on the next page how many "b's"...it gets a bit boring really......

Action plans for successful learning

- Monitor all young readers, and take special notice of those who seem to need more input and make slower progress than their peers.

- Be quick to pick up early reading difficulties to prevent loss of confidence and frustration at the very early stages of reading.

- Regularly review all students to check on the development of their reading.

- Do not assume that because a student does well with silent reading comprehension, the accuracy is equally good. Check for reading accuracy as well as comprehension.

- Ensure that there are plenty of tasks that do not depend on strong reading skills. Interviews, videos, films, audio tapes, and practical learning can all be the starting point of a valuable learning activity.

- Offer alternative assessments that do not depend on skilled reading. For example, administer oral tests instead of written tests.

- Make suitable reading materials available for students whose interest level is in advance of their reading skills.

- Avoid asking students to read out loud in class unless they wish to do so.

- Provide an appropriate remedial reading program to improve skills.

- Modify curriculum materials so that the content remains the same but the level of reading required is reduced; supplement easy-to-read words, short sentences, etc.

- Check the reading difficulty level of curriculum materials by using the readability statistics option on your computer grammar check.

- Make worksheets and homework sheets physically easy to read.

  - Use good quality photocopies.
  - Print information in a large font (minimum point size 12).
  - Use a clear font such as Arial, Times New Roman, or Comic Sans.
  - Leave plenty of space around each item.
  - Draw attention to particularly important information by using graphics and special effects.
  - Use tinted or off white paper.
  - If teacher-created assignments and tests need to be handwritten, be sure to write in clear print.

- Allow extra time for completion of seat work. This may necessitate reducing the work load to avoid increasing the overall time a student is expected to work.

- If extra time cannot be allowed for assignment completion, shorten the assignment to take into account the slow reading speed. If the assignment begins with easy items and moves on to more challenging questions, have the student do alternate items and then go back (if there is time) to fill in missed questions. The student will then have a good mixture of easy and difficult items.

- Assign a partner to read essential information to the student with dyslexia.

- Allow reading to be shared between the student with dyslexia and a more skilled reader.

- Supplement printed material with demonstrations, verbal explanations, and diagrams.

- Provide essential information in an alternative form (diagrams, audio tapes, or videos).

- Provide a resource folder to help students with the current curriculum. Compile the following from current students to use with students in the upcoming years:

  o   Copies of relevant reading
  o   Abbreviated notes
  o   Highlighted text and diagrams
  o   Illustrations
  o   Video
  o   Suggested topic headings
  o   Outlines

- Put curriculum materials on disc or scan textbooks, information sheets, worksheets, or test papers into the computer and use text-to-speech software. If writing for text-to-speech software:

  o   Use punctuation at the end of headings and bullet point items.
  o   Use numbered items to ease navigation.
  o   Use short sentences and paragraphs.
  o   Use lower case letters.

- Use a text scanner that can scan individual words and provide a read-out.

RECOGNIZING COMMONLY USED WORDS

When students with dyslexia read, they often lack automatic word recognition. This means, that almost every word they come across has to be worked out from scratch, over and over again, each time it is encountered.

Printed words are usually easy to remember when they are visually distinctive and have an interesting meaning: *spaghetti, elephant,* and *zebra* all look distinctive and have real meaning; therefore, most young readers find them quite easy to remember.

In contrast, words such as *where, here, he, they, the, then,* etc., are visually similar, have no interesting meaning and are very difficult to recall. As adults, we sometimes think these words should be easy because they are used so often. For students with dyslexia, however, they often prove to be the most difficult and frustrating words of all. Remember that matching and recognizing words are easier tasks than reading words at sight.

Action plans for successful learning

- Introduce beginning readers to sight words by matching and recognizing activities before reading is required. Matching to sample is the easiest level; reading words is the most difficult.

    o Match to sample (sample in view):

    This technique teaches the student to discriminate between print patterns.

    Choose three to five different words. Write each word five times on separate cards. Spread the cards out on the table.

    Choose one word card and hold it up for the student to see.

    Say: "This card says 'house'. Find another card that says 'house'."

    o Match to sample (sample hidden):

    This technique teaches the student to hold a mental image of a printed word.

    Choose three to five different words. Write each word five times on separate cards. Spread the cards out on the table.

    Choose one word card and hold it up for the student to see.

    Say: "Look at this word. It says 'who.' Remember what it looks like because I am going to turn it over." Place the card face down.

    Say: "Find another card that says 'who.' "

    o Recognize a named word:

    This technique teaches the student to link a printed word with a spoken word.

    Choose three to five different words. Write each word five times on separate cards. Spread the cards out on the table.

    Say: "Find the word that says 'out' for me. Find the word that says 'my' for me."

    o   Read words at sight:

        This is the most difficult level. The student is asked to remember a print pattern from previous learning and to name the word.

        Choose three to five different words. Write each word five times on separate cards. Spread the cards out on the table.

        Point to the words in turn and say, "What does this word say?"

- Use games such as Word Lotto®, Word Snap®, and matching games to help develop quick, automatic recall of words.

- Use flash cards regularly to promote quick automatic recall of printed words.

> Remember that words like these are really hard to tell apart and difficult to remember:
>
> *where   here   he   the   we   what   were   there   is   they   their   she   and*

- For the emergent reader, use match-to-sample sentence building to teach word recognition and sentence structure.

    o   Write an interesting sentence on a blank sentence strip. Make an exact duplicate of the sentence and cut it into individual words. Give the student the word cards from the cut-up strip.

    o   Say: "Look, this sentence says 'It is my birthday on Saturday.' Put your cards down so that they say 'It is my birthday on Saturday.' "

    o   Encourage the student to use the complete sentence as a guide. Make sure that the students read their sentence to you once they are complete.

- For the student who already knows a few sight words, use sentence building to strengthen word recognition and sentence structure. This activity helps students constantly review the core sight words.

    o   Have a set of words on individual cards. Magnetic Poetry® (available from many bookstores) provides interesting word sets. The words will stick to file cabinets, refrigerators, or any metal surface.

        Say: "Put these cards together to a make a sentence."

o   You can either dictate a sentence or the more advanced student can choose words from the set to make their own.

> Try words like these to build a young readers confidence:
> *tyrannosaurus rex   pizza   Sesame Street   giraffe   chocolate   banana*
> *Scooby Doo   whopper   elephant   STOP   spaghetti   Lego   Lion King*

- Create personal reading material related to the student's interests by using the student's name. For younger students, create language experience stories. Also include sight words that are difficult to remember.

- Use reading materials that are in a well structured series to provide repetition and a controlled level of difficulty.

- Avoid relying on randomly selected books (even if the books are sorted according to difficulty). Select books that control the introduction of new words and consolidate previously introduced words.

- Use reading books which have supplementary material (such as workbooks, parallel readers, flash cards, and supplemental extension activities) associated with them.

- Make one reading book the core of a range of literacy activities such as:

  o   Homemade readers which reintroduce words from the reader
  o   Sentence-building activities to give extra practice with the new words
  o   Word games to build familiarity with the new words

- Give daily reading practice.

LEARNING LETTERS AND SOUNDS

Learning letters and their associated sounds is the beginning point for successful reading and spelling. Sometimes, delay in this learning is due to poor memory, but more often it is due to underdeveloped phonological awareness. If the student does not recognize individual sounds in words, then learning printed symbols to represent those sounds makes no sense at all. The first step is to provide training in awareness of sounds in speech and spelling. (See pages 36 - 41)

Learning the relationship between letters and sounds is a difficult type of learning because neither the individual sound or the individual letter have meaning to the young student.

Teacher holding up the letter **S**: *"Ben, what does this letter say?"*
Ben: *"I never heard it say nothing."*

Learning letters and sounds is a complex task of integration between the language channel (which handles the sounds) and the visual or visual motor channel (which handles the written letters).

Action plans for successful learning

- Before you can teach the link between printed letters and sounds, you must make sure that the students can at least tell the initial sounds in words. If they cannot do this, then continue to work at basic phonological awareness activities. (See page 36.)

- Match letters to pictures on the basis of initial sounds.

- Use more than one word/picture for each letter sound to teach that **S** is not just associated with *sun* but also goes with *snake, sand, sausage*, etc.

- Use a multisensory approach so that students learn through sight, touch, and sound. Students can practice making their letter shapes by tracing the letter with their fingertip in wet sand, icing, shaving cream, or sugar sprinkled on a baking tray. It is important that the student is encouraged to simultaneously say the sound as the letter is being formed.

- Do not teach letters that sound similar at the same time. Avoid introducing **S** with **Z** or **m** with **n**, as they are so easily confused.

- Do not teach letters that look similar to each other at the same time. Avoid introducing letters **f** and **t**, or the letters **b** and **d** at the same time as they are easily confused.

- Ask parents and classroom volunteers to use only sounds to avoid confusion between letter names and sounds. Teach letters and their sounds in stages.

Teach letters and their sounds in stages.

Matching

You will need two sets of letters. Hold up a letter and give the sound. For example, hold up the letter "**S.**"

Say: "This is '**SSSS**'. Find another '**SSSS**' ".

Students with very limited letter-sound knowledge should be given only two or three letters to choose from to make their match. As students gain confidence, they can be given more letters to choose from.

Recognize

This is slightly harder, because the student is not given a sample or its sound to start. Instead, the adult scatters some letters in front of the student and asks: "Find a **t**" (or whatever letter the adult wants to work on). Once again, young students who do not have a full repertoire of letters and sounds established should only be given a few multiple copies of the same letter within their set, so that they can have repeated practice.

Read

At this level the students are not given a sample and is not given a target sound to find. Instead they are shown a letter and asked: "What is the sound of this letter?"

Record

This is the most difficult level of all. The student hears the sound and is asked to write it down. For example, say: "Write down the letter that makes the **mmm** sound."

- Provide an illustrated alphabet strip or chart to help the student remember the letters that match each sound.

USING PHONICS IN READING

One of the most common characteristics of a student with dyslexia is difficulty in using phonics for reading. The process of linking letters with sounds and then stringing the sounds together to make words is a challenging one for the student with dyslexia.

Students may be very confident in giving the sounds of each individual letter, but when it is necessary to blend the sounds, they are lost. For example, the student may sound out "skin" but think that the word is "sick" or "snick."

All readers have to master the skill of recognizing clusters of letters within long words. These "chunks" are easier to work with than are strings of individual letters.

It is usually essential for the student with dyslexia to have intensive and explicit instruction with regards to phonics. This type of input is often required for a number of years until the basics are fully established.

Action plans for successful learning

- Assess the student's current ability to sound words out using phonics and decide if remedial input is required. If so, establish an appropriate starting point.

- Use one of the highly structured phonics programs especially written for students with reading difficulties. It is essential that the program teaches phonics in an explicit and highly structured way. The International Dyslexia Association and the British Dyslexia Association have information about recommended programs. Well respected programs include Hickey, Orton Gillingham, and Spalding.

- Select a reading program that has a high phonic content and is structured to provide graduated practice in phonics.

- Work from easy to difficult phonic patterns.

Suggested sequence of instruction for teaching phonics:

1. Three-letter words which form consonant-vowel-consonant pattern sounds: *hot, jam, mud, top*
2. Four-letter words, where two letters slide together to make a sound: *flag, step, best, tick*
3. Four-letter words where two consonants make a new sound: *shop, thin, chat, when*
4. Four-letter words where a vowel and a consonant make a new sound: *corn, fowl, warm, quit*
5. Four-letter words with a final "*e*": *mice, date, kite, made*
6. Three- and four-letter words where two vowels make a new sound: *rain, out, loud, meat*
7. Silent letters: *knee gnaw, gnat, know*
8. Five-letter words where three letters slide together: *strap, scrum, strip, judge, squid*
9. Five- and six-letter words where four letters make a new sound: *fight, dough, nation*

10. Longer words that combine two or more of the previous patterns: *jumper, beach, sprawl, tribe*

11. Prefixes, suffixes, and compound words: *predict, disagree, truthfully, household*

- Teaching a student with dyslexia requires considerable skill. A qualified special education teacher should plan and implement the appropriate program.

- Teach groups of words with the same phonic clusters together to consolidate awareness:

  pain, rain, gain, or gate, hate, mate, fate

- Use nonsense words as well as real words to give additional practice and to challenge phonic skills.

- Work from short words to longer words. Do not use long words to teach basic phonics. If teaching "**st**", use only four-letter words such as stop, step, and list, and not words such as steamer, string, or beast. The longer words have additional phonic challenges which will confuse the student.

- Give auditory blending activities. The student listens to strings of sounds and says the word.

Say: "I am going to say some sounds slowly. You put them together to make a word."

Sample words
t – ap
s – un
m – a – n
b – e – g
fl – a – g
st – a – mp
cr – a – sh

If this is difficult for the student, use picture prompts. The adult sounds out the names of objects which are illustrated on cards. The students select the picture that goes with the word they have just heard.

- Give modeled practice. The adult prepares a list of words. The adult sounds out the first word and says the whole word "c-u-p, cup." The student is then asked to repeat the process in exactly the same way (first sounding the letters and then saying the whole word). The adult moves to the next word on the list and repeats the procedure. Once the list has been worked through, the student is asked to go back to the beginning and sound and blend the words alone.

- Give plenty of guided practice (the student practices and the adult guides) in the use of phonics for reading.

- Once basic phonics have been mastered, teach the rules for syllable division and provide plenty of explicit practice in this skill. Use both real and nonsense words to develop skills.

- Return to the basics frequently to check for mastery and (if necessary) review, because students with dyslexia readily lose previously established skills.

- Use analogy reading to encourage the development of the ability to use one word to help with another. If this says "*tease*." then that word says…….. (*please*).

- Accelerate word decoding with phonics by giving short, intensive "sound-and-say"   drills. Word cards are dealt out quickly and the student is asked to sound and say the words as fast as possible.

- Write down pairs of words that look quite similar: *girl grill, red read, pair pure.* Name one of each pair for the student to find: "*Which word says grill?*"

READING FLUENCY

Once the student with dyslexia has mastered the skills in sounding out new words and recognizes the most commonly used words by sight, there may still be significant problems in developing fluent, confident reading. Reading may be slow and stilted, so that meaning is often lost and reading becomes a real chore. Although this lack of automatic reading is often part of the student's difficulty, jerky, hesitant reading can sometimes be a habit stemming from earlier difficulties.

> Margo, an adult with dyslexia, recalls her school days:
>
> *Usually I never got asked to read to the class, but one teacher she got me reading the prayers all the time. 'Margo', she'd say, 'You read the prayer, it sounds so reverent the way you do it' I reckon it was only because I was so darned slow...couldn't have gone any faster if I tried!*

Many students can read reasonably successfully, but reading still takes a long time. Some words may have to be decoded, and the text may need to be read several times before it is fully understood. Students with dyslexia often fail to finish reading because they run out of time.

Hesitant reading can also be a characteristic of a student with a word-finding problem. If this is so, then a similar hesitancy will probably be occasionally noticed in ordinary conversation.

Action plans for successful learning

- Give intensive, supported practice to improve reading skills and speed.

- Select reading books that have a large percentage of familiar words.

- Select sequential reading books from a series, so that core vocabulary, style, font type, etc., are consistent and the introduction of new words is controlled.

- Encourage the rereading of previously enjoyed books.

- Pre-read new books to the students so that they have an overview and understand the story before they start to read for themselves.

- Encourage the student to look through a new book to become familiar with it before starting to read.

- Use modeled reading, in which the adult reads a sentence or a small section with expression and then the student reads the modeled reading as closely as possible.

- Use a highlighter pen to mark each sentence into phrases in order to give the student guided practice in reading in phrases instead of words. For example, instead of reading: *Once – upon – a – time – there – was – a – wicked – king – who – had –a beautiful – daughter* read *Once upon a time - there was a wicked king - who had a beautiful daughter.*

- Select books which are short in length but of high interest to the student.

- Record the student during reading and let the student listen to the playback. Continue recording until the student feels comfortable with the audiotape. Keep the first tapes for the student to hear the improvement.

- Use timed reading. The student prepares, rehearses, and practices reading the same passage until fluent and accurate. Time the first read-through and note time taken and errors made. Repeat the process, aiming for reduction in time and errors. The student might like to calculate the reading rate (words per minute).

- Try choral reading where a small group of students rehearse a poem or short story as a dramatic presentation. The readers read in unison and rehearse until their reading is fluent and expressive.

- Introduce humor, drama, or excitement into individual reading. Have students:

  o Rehearse reading a comedy routine of good jokes or stories and perform them to friends.
  o Practice for a part in a short play, and perform the play for fun (have the script stuck around the stage or use big cue cards to give the performers their words).
  o Practice reading a story and then audiotape it for another student to enjoy.
  o Read a news flash like a TV anchor and have the auto cue on the screen of a computer.
  o Practice reading a book at school and then take the book home. Read the book fluently to parents, siblings, or grandparents.

- Assess the student's reading both in silent and oral modes. Poor oral reading may be due to word-finding difficulties, not reading difficulties.

- Avoid asking the student read aloud in front of peers.

- If the student must read aloud in front of peers, give time and support for rehearsal.

- Reduce the volume of reading required by highlighting important sections, or setting only selected chapters, chapter summaries, or shorter sections to be read.

- Share reading with a skilled reader so that the reading process is speeded up by taking turns.

- Use paired reading, where the student reads in tandem with a skilled reader. The skilled reader sets the pace a little faster than the usual speed of the student with dyslexia. This can help with the transition from word-by-word reading to fluent, expressive reading.

- Use books on audiotape so the student is able to read along. Take care that the book is an exact match for the printed text and that the speed is appropriate.

- Allow sufficient time for essential reading to be completed properly.

- Avoid overloading the student with reading requirements.

- Allow the student extra time in tests and examinations to take account of slow reading speed.

- Provide supplementary information such as diagrams to convey information more quickly.

READING COMPREHENSION

Students with dyslexia often have quite good reading comprehension provided they can read the text fluently and accurately enough to be able to focus on the meaning of the words. Poor comprehension is often associated with books that are too difficult to read.

Some students do have subtle language problems that will interfere with their reading comprehension.

Action plans for successful learning

- Obtain advice and support from a speech therapist if it is felt that the student has general language difficulties.

- Monitor the readability of books. Check that any book the students are attempting to read is within their range of reading skill.

- Give the student a brief summary of the book before reading begins to ensure that the student has an overview of the theme or story line.

- Choose books with plenty of illustrations to support comprehension.

- Encourage rereading the book. The first read-through is to work out the actual words and the second read-through is for understanding.

- Preread the book to the student with dyslexia before the student reads it alone.

- Talk about the book and ask questions to check for comprehension. If the student's comprehension is uncertain, check for understanding by offering two alternatives. For example, "Did they go to the park or the beach?" instead of "Where did they go?"

- Ask the student to locate information to develop comprehension. For example: "Find the part that tells us how Tom was feeling."

- Check to be sure that the book's language is not too advanced for the student.

- Ask the student to devise reading-comprehension questions for other readers. This will encourage the student to think about the meaning of the reading.

- Encourage reading for meaning by deleting words from text. Ask the student to predict the missing words.

- Have the student draw a cartoon style strip to retell the story.

- Teach the student how to use the words of the question to guide the answer. If the question is "Why did Harry hate going to school?," the answer could begin "Harry hated school because…"

- Ask the student to select the best answer to comprehension questions from a choice of two or three possible options. Why did the chicken cross the road? a) *Roast chicken tastes better than fried chicken* b) *She wanted to get to the other side* c) *She was afraid of the dark.*

- Teach students to listen for key words in questions. A *why* question usually has a because answer. A *where* question often has an in, on, by, near, or at in the answer. A *when* question usually has after, before, when, on, or at in the answer.

SUSTAINED READING

For the student with dyslexia, reading can be a real struggle and just reading a few lines can take a lot of effort. Students with dyslexia often find sustained reading very difficult. The student may read for a short period of time but quickly become exhausted by the effort required. This means that the student often finds it difficult to enjoy a book. They read a little and then stop because they are already tired. Often it is difficult for the student to really get into, understand, enjoy, and finish an entire book.

Quick onset of fatigue when reading can also be related to visual difficulties not connected with dyslexia

Action plans for successful learning

- Arrange for eyesight to be tested.

- Do not expect skilled reading when the student with dyslexia is already tired.

- Help the student to structure the reading into short, manageable sections.

- Locate books that have short chapters, but include interesting stories or information.

- Assist with reading by sharing the load; take turns to read a paragraph, or alternate pages.

- Start a new book by reading the first chapter or two together to get the student interested and excited to read on.

- Find books that follow an already familiar story. For example, select a book the student has already viewed in video form.

- Find a time for reading when the student is free from distraction.

VISUAL TRACKING

To track along a line of print, drop accurately to the next line of print, and continue tracking word by word is a very refined skill. Some students have difficulties with this. In its extreme form, it would be described as ocular-motor dyspraxia.

Some students with scanning difficulties will attempt to scan the print by moving their heads and keeping their eyes static. Others will constantly lose their places when reading or copying.

Action plans for successful learning

- Encourage the parent(s) to arrange for an appointment with an optometrist or ophthalmologist with specific reference to ocular movements (scanning).

- Use a piece of plain card to underline the line of print which is being read.

- Provide enlarged text which is double spaced.

- Rest the book on a sloping surface rather than on a flat surface.

- Put reading material on a computer, and use the cursor as a pointer.

- Project text onto a flat, vertical surface at a distance to allow for less precise eye movements.

- Simplify worksheets so that the text is well spread out and clear to read.

WANTING TO READ

Students with dyslexia often avoid reading whenever possible, perhaps hiding or "losing" books to avoid reading practice. Some students claim to be ill, volunteer to do errands, or behave badly to get themselves outside of the classroom when it is time to read. Some students with dyslexia become anxious and agitated when they have to read; others may become tearful, angry, or upset. This may mean that reading practice is limited, which further compounds the problem. Students with dyslexia who are still acquiring basic reading skills should read to an adult daily.

The emotional and social consequences of dyslexia are discussed in detail in Chapter 8.

Action plans for successful learning

- Teach, don't test. Give as much help as the student needs to read successfully. Tell the student unfamiliar words, help with sounding out, or read alongside the student to get through difficult parts.

- Make sure that the book being read is at a reasonable level of difficulty. The student should be able to read at least nine words out of ten for comfortable reading.

- Set up a relaxed atmosphere for reading. Curl up on a couch or comfortable chair; have a supply of treats reserved only for reading time. Enjoy the book by looking at the pictures and talking about associated topics, as well as actually reading the words.

- Suggest that the students use a signal (such as raising a finger or tapping on the table) to indicate that they need help with a particular word.

- When listening to the student read, if the student gets stuck on a word, allow a silent count of four seconds for the student to sound out the word. After the four-second wait time, simply sound the word out and say the word. For example say: *l-ou-d, loud* and allow the student to continue reading.

- If the word will not sound out, just say the word aloud and let the student continue reading.

- If the student makes a mistake, but the word used makes sense, let the reading continue without comment.

- If the student is confused when reading, go back to the beginning of the sentence and start the student off again. Read along if the student needs extra help.

- Some adults let their own anxieties or impatience show through, which in turn makes the students very nervous when they read. In this situation, find an alternative person to listen to the student read.

- Keep reading sessions short and let the students know how long the session will last, so that they do not feel trapped for an indeterminate time. "We will read until the buzzer goes. Then we will stop."

- Make sure that the adults keep track of the books the student has read and also monitor how often the student reads. Good communication between home and school is important to prevent avoidance tactics.

- Reading without preparation can be very threatening. Allow the students to preview the book and say when they are ready to read.

- Do not assume that the student will actually read during class reading time. Make this a time for reading to an adult or provide reading-based activities such as crossword puzzles, multiple-choice quizzes, cloze activities, etc., to give interactive reading practice.

- Find low readability, high interest books that will appeal to the student. Books of amazing facts, world records, or jokes are popular. The short segments of reading really can be enjoyed.

- Record favorite TV shows to be watched after reading is completed.

- Make daily reading practice a homework assignment in place of another, less important task. Do not make the student do reading as an extra chore on top of the regular work load.

- Model enjoyment in reading. Let the student see that adults read for information and pleasure.

- Create a reward system for reading, so that the hard work involved has a tangible, positive outcome

- Make a "*Lucky Dip*". Write various rewards on slips of paper and put them in a jar. This reward can be used both at school and at home.

  School:
  - Ten extra minutes of free time during class
  - Ten minutes of additional computer time
  - Skip one homework assignment (teacher must approve)
  - Select a candy from the candy jar.

  Home:
  - Get a chocolate frog from the box
  - 10 minutes extra TV before you go to bed
  - Your choice of dessert tonight
  - 50 cents for you

- Draw a grid of a 10x10 squares. Each square represents 1 minute of reading. If the student reads for four minutes, the student colors in four squares. Small rewards can be given for completing each line of 10 squares and a larger reward can be given when the entire square is complete (100 minutes of reading). For really reluctant readers, put in some bonus squares. When they reach or exceed the bonus square, that session's minutes are doubled.

- Get students excited to read by making reading a fundraiser for a favorite charity or a school project. Make sure the student with dyslexia has a reasonable goal. For example, the majority of students may be sponsored by the book, whereas the student with dyslexia may be sponsored by the page.

- Allow reading time to be offset against household chores. For example, reading for 20 minutes cancels out cleaning their bedroom, cleaning up the kitchen, or any other regularly scheduled chore.

Chapter 3

LANGUAGE AND DYSLEXIA

LANGUAGE SKILLS

AWARENESS OF SOUNDS IN SPEECH AND SPELLING

WORD FINDING

LANGUAGE SKILLS

Most contemporary definitions of dyslexia describe dyslexia as a fundamental difficulty with language-based skills. The neurological process of linking auditory information (spoken words) with visual information (printed words) is extraordinarily complex. It is not surprising that difficulties sometimes occur in the development of the pathways and connections that underpin the ability to use language, to read, and to write.

Research studies consistently demonstrate that most dyslexic students have a disorder in their ability to process language. This difficulty may often be at a very subtle level, but nevertheless, it has a profound impact on the ability to read and write.

We also know that children who are late learning to talk or who have disordered early language are at higher risk of having dyslexia than children who have had no early language difficulties. Indeed, dyslexia may sometimes be seen as a residual of earlier language problems. More overt language difficulties may clear up through maturity and therapy, but subtle processing problems often continue.

We know that young children who have a history of recurrent ear infections seem to be at greater risk of dyslexia than children who have had few, if any, ear infections. The probability is that there is already a risk factor, but the disruption of the child's auditory processing development in the critical early years leads to continued difficulties as the child grows older.

It is also known that speech, language, and phonological difficulties have a genetic component. It may often be that several children in the same family, or several members of the same family, all have similar language-related learning difficulties.

Action plans for successful learning

- Ask parents about earlier speech and language difficulties as part of your school enrollment procedure.

- Ask parents about their child's history of ear infections and intermittent hearing difficulties as a preschooler as part of your school enrollment policy.

- Ask parents about their family history of speech, language, and literacy difficulties as part of your school enrollment procedure.

- View any students with a history of speech and language difficulties as "at risk" of literacy problems in their early years of schooling.

- Monitor students with a history of speech, language or hearing difficulties for continuing, more subtle language difficulties (such as delay in the development of phonological awareness) which may impact their learning at school.

- Give all new school entrants a basic screening test of phonological awareness and language skills.

- Arrange for an assessment by a speech pathologist and/or a psychologist who specializes in language/literacy disorders if you are concerned about a particular student.

AWARENESS OF SOUNDS IN SPEECH AND SPELLING

The process of acquiring spoken language is based on the ability to hear segments of speech (phonemes) within words and the ability to manipulate these sounds. Babies babble as they practice the phonemes in their language; older children love to play with phonemes by making up nonsense rhymes. This ability to recognize and deal with phonemes will play a central part in the early stages of literacy acquisition. Children with early difficulties in establishing these basics will be delayed in their readiness to work with phonemes when they start to learn to read and write.

Phonological awareness is the ability to recognize individual sounds within words and to recognize the number and position of these sounds. Phonological awareness is a critical beginning point for correct spelling. Without recognizing the sounds within words, the student cannot use letters to represent those sounds to write a word down. The student has to be able to recognize the number of sounds within the word and the order in which those sounds occur. They also, of course, have to know the letters which represent those sounds.

Sensitivity to the sequence of sounds is also a very important aspect of phonological awareness. Difficulties sequencing of sounds leads to problems with pronunciation. The student may say hostipal instead of hospital; in turn, this will lead to spelling problems.

On the Weekn my fren is uning oft.
riding is verg esnfr
Spllie is Vergesnfr

This student has not yet developed adequate phonological awareness to underpin accurate spelling. She has written:

On the weekend my friend is coming over.
Reading is very easy.
Spelling is very easy.

Action plans for successful learning

- Start teaching phonological awareness activities at the oral level, followed by a "hands on," physical manipulation of letters, and writing words.

Oral

At the oral stage, nothing is written down at all. The aim at this level is to help the student become aware that speech is split up into words and that the words can be split up into sounds (phonemes).

- Word counting. The adult says sentences and phrases, and the student has to count the words.

Ask the student: "How many words do you hear?"

Sample phrases and words:
  o *Poor bear*
  o *Brightly colored beads*
  o *Pitter patter pitter patter*
  o *I can see stars.*
  o *I love chocolate pudding.*
  o *Who has been eating my porridge?*

- Finding the missing word. The student listens to a list of words and notices the missing word. Begin with two words and then increase the length of the list.

  Say to the student: "Listen to the words I say: flowers, apples, spoon. Now I am going to say them again. Tell me which word is left out : apple, spoon."

  > ***Sample word lists:***
  > - *window (dog)*
  > - *(flower) laugh house*
  > - *road book pen (cup)*
  > - *boy (girl) baby mother*

- Rhyming words. The student recognizes and produces rhymes.

  Level 1: Rhyming sequences. Say to the student: "Tell me the word that comes next: rat, bat, sat…"

  > ***Sample sequences to complete***
  > - *rose, nose, those, . . .*
  > - *head, red, led, . . .*
  > - *tree, me, he, . . .*
  > - *hit, fit, pit, . . .*

  Level 2: Rhyming words. Say to the student: "Tell me a word that rhymes with house."

  > ***Sample words for rhymes***
  > - *play*
  > - *top*
  > - *inner*
  > - *socks*

- Clapping syllables. The student listens to words and recognizes syllables.

  Say to the student: "We are going to clap and count syllables. Sun has one syllable." (clap and say sun) "Sunshine has two syllables." (clap on both syllables of sunshine.)

> **Sample words**
> o   *leg*
> o   *rocket*
> o   *sister*
> o   *toy*
> o   *caravan*

- Phoneme deletion. The student listens to words and deletes phonemes.

  Say to the student: "We are going to say words and then take part of the word away. Say 'sunshine.' Now say it again without the 'sun.' "

> **Sample words**
> o   *teapot without the tea*
> o   *telephone without the phone*
> o   *classroom without the class*
> o   *cup without the* **c**
> o   *room without the* **m**

- Play "I-Spy." Select three or four items which have distinct initial sounds. Place the items on a tray, and play at "I-Spy" using letter sounds (not names). Say: "I spy with my little eye something beginning with **SSSS**."

> **Sample items for tray**
> o   *pencil, flower, box, soap*
> o   *horse cow, duck, farmer*
> o   *apple, banana, cracker, marshmallow*

- Give riddles that have an initial sound as a clue. Remember to say the sound that the letter makes.

> **Sample riddles:**
> o   *An animal that you can ride. It starts with* **d** *sound (donkey)*
> o   *A fruit that is yellow. It starts with* **b** *sound (banana)*
> o   *Something that you wear. It starts with* **h** *sound (hat)*

- Talk about words, and identify the first sound in spoken words: "What is the first sound in bell?"

- Give the student two or three individual consonants written on separate cards. Say three-letter words and ask the students to point to the sound they heard at the beginning of each word.

  Say: "Listen to this word. What sound comes first? Show me the letter."

- Choose a word. Take turns to think of another word that has the same sound.

- Recognize initial sounds in words, and match the sound to the correct letter. Give the student two or three individual consonants written on separate cards plus one blank card. Place these cards on the table. Give the student a set of pictures.

  Say: "Put these pictures by the right letter. See, here is a picture of a house, that goes with the **h** card. This is a bird. There is no **b** card so we will put in on the blank card."

- Once the student is accurate with the initial sounds, start to work with final sounds in three-letter words

- Play "I-Spy" with final sounds. Say: "I Spy with my little eye, something that ends with **t**."

- Recognize final sounds and match the sound to the correct letter. Give the student two or three individual consonants written on separate cards plus one blank card. Place these cards on the table. Give the student a set of pictures.

  Say: "Put these pictures by the right letter. Here is cat. Cat ends with t so that goes with the **t** card. This is a dog. There is no **G** card so we will put in on the blank card."

- Give the student two or three individual consonants written on separate cards. Say three-letter words and ask the student to point to the sound they heard at the end of each word.

  Say: "Listen to this word. What sound comes at the end of the word? Show me the letter."

- Middle (medial) sounds are the hardest, and these are introduced once the student is confident in recognizing first and final sounds.

• Give the student two or three individual vowels written on separate cards. Say three-letter words and ask the student to point to the sound they heard in the middle of each word.

Say: "Listen to this word. What sound comes in the middle? Show me the letter."

• Saying sounds in words. The student has to identify each sound in order. For example, the sounds in wet are w-e-t.

Say: "Tell me the sounds in this word." Start with simple CVC (consonant vowel consonant) words.

Samples of CVC words
o wet
o tom
o hip

Samples of CCVC words
o flag
o twin
o step

Samples of CVCC words
o best
o mend
o mint

Concrete

While working at the oral level, begin to introduce plastic letters (lower case), to help the dyslexic student to learn to manipulate sounds and place them in the correct order.

• Word building. Choose a three-letter word, for example pig. Give the student only the letters needed to create the word.

Say: "Look, I can make the word pig with these letters. p-i-g, pig."

Once you have made the word, scramble the letters and move them towards the student.

Say: "Now you make the word 'pig.' "

Encourage the student to say the sounds as the letters are placed in order. If the student is not sure what to do, put the first letter in place, and ask the student to complete the word.

- Once the student is confident, do not give an example. Just provide the letters needed for a word and ask the student to place the letters correctly. Always encourage the student to sound out the word as the letters are placed.

- When the students can build three-letter words with the letters provided, give them a larger set of letters to choose from. For a three-letter word such as hat, give five letters such as h,j,a,e,t so that the student has to make choices about what sounds are needed.

- When three-letter words are mastered move to four-letter words with a consonant blend: flag, twin, best, mend

- Swapping sounds. The student builds a word with plastic letters and then has to take one letter away and replace it with another to make a new word.

  Say: "Make the word 'pig' with the letters. Change 'pig' into 'wig.'" Take one letter away and find another to make 'wig.' "

Sample words (initial sounds)
- o *change dad to mad*
- o *change cat to hat*
- o *change tin to pin*

Sample words (final sounds)
- o *change dog to dot*
- o *change hit to him*
- o *change peg to pen*

Sample words (middle sounds)
- o *change him to ham*
- o *change cat to cut*
- o *change tip to top*

WORD FINDING

Many students with dyslexia have difficulties with "word finding". The words that they need are within their vocabulary, but they experience difficulties in 'finding' those words when they are needed. The student with the word-finding difficulty may often seem to talk quite a lot, but close listening will show that they may be substituting words, hesitating and using 'fillers' such as, "ah", "ur", and "you know". As preschoolers, they may have been slow at learning to name colors, and may continue to have difficulties in naming things quickly. Many studies show that difficulty in rapid naming is one of the most common characteristics of dyslexia.

> Looking for the missing details in pictures is easy, but these details are hard to name if you have a word-finding problem.
>
> *The stick thing (handle of a broom)*
> *The bit...the thing that you stand on (the step of a ladder)*
> *The watch what goes round thing (the watch band)*
> *You know the thingy...the thingy...that's a thingy bit that you pull (the handle on a drawer)*

Students with word-finding difficulties will often seem to perform erratically in the classroom. The students will raise their hands and will be eager to answer, but when asked to make their contribution, the students may "forget" what they were going to say.

Word-finding difficulties are often much worse when the student is tired or upset. In disputes or disagreements with other students, the student with the word-finding difficulty may have significant problems negotiating verbally. The student may be more likely to communicate physically and frequently will have more difficulty in explaining to an adult what has happened.

Students with word-finding problems are also likely to have problems with reading fluency. They may recognize the word and understand what it means, but experience difficulties 'finding' the right word to say out loud. The process of word finding has to be quick and automatic for fluent oral reading to occur. Students with word finding difficulties may often have particular difficulties with oral reading, and may be much more accurate when they read silently.

> **Action plans for successful learning**
>
> • If word-finding difficulties are observed, arrange for a speech pathologist to assess and ask for advice.

- When students are speaking, give them plenty of time to "find" the words that they need.

- If the student offers an answer but then cannot remember what they were going to say, offer them a way out. Say: "Were you going to say the animal in the story was a camel?"

- Rehearse assertive statements such as: Stop it! I do not like it. or You are breaking the rules. to give the student with word-finding difficulties phrases that come easily, even when upset.

- When an upset has occurred, allow the students time to calm down. Let the students tell their side of the story without interruptions from others.

- Encourage the students to write down the answer before they raise their hand to answer a question.

- Do not judge a student's arithmetic by oral answers, as word-finding difficulties may disguise their capabilities.

- Check reading accuracy and comprehension using silent reading and oral reading. A student with a word-finding difficulty may be much better at silent reading.

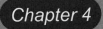

Chapter 4

WRITING AND SPELLING

REMEMBERING HOW TO SPELL WORDS

Students with dyslexia frequently have major difficulties in remembering spelling words that they have learned. They may obtain a high score in a weekly spelling test, but their overall spelling in their own writing is poor. They can learn spelling "parrot fashion" for a test, but often do not retain this spelling. Many students with dyslexia follow a "learn and forget" pattern of spelling (learn the words for Friday, forget them by Monday, start learning the new set, and repeat the process time and time again).

Students with this type of memory difficulty often have to reinvent the same word over and over again each time they try to use it in their own writing. The spelling patterns which they have learned have not progressed to automatic recall.

Although accurate spelling is important, we have to remember that quality writing does not depend on correct spelling. Students with dyslexia who are made to feel overly anxious about their spelling may restrict what they write to avoid spelling errors. They may seriously reduce the overall quality of their work in doing so.

Action plans for successful learning

- Separate good writing from good spelling. Always give credit for creativity, expressive vocabulary, interesting information, innovative ideas, good thinking, and evidence of good research.

- Sort words into those that can be learned phonetically and words that are irregular.

Action plans for successful learning of phonically regular words

- Check that the student can recognize sounds in words. To begin spelling phonetically, the student should be able to tell the individual sounds in three-letter words. (See page 39.)

- Check that the student knows how to write the correct letter for each sound.

- Place an alphabet strip on the desk so that the student can refer it as needed. For some students, a picture prompt with each letter will help create the link between sound and letter.

- Start by building a word with plastic letters. (See page 40.) Allow the students to sound out the word until they are confident they can remember it. Scramble the letters and ask students to write the word. Encourage students to repeat the sounding-out process to assist with the recall of the phonetic pattern.

- Teach the student to make a habit of trying to say the sounds before starting to write a word. This helps to reinforce the development of phonological awareness and significantly increases spelling accuracy

  (See page 21 for a suggested sequence for the introduction of phonetic patterns.)

- When teaching phonics for spelling, focus on the blend being taught. For instance, if teaching "ou," stay with three- and four-letter words (for example out and loud).   Do not introduce longer words (such as shouted) because these words have additional complexities which make it harder for the student to hear the sounds correctly.

- When introducing new words always emphasize the phonetic structure of the word. Teach the student to split the word into phonemes (units of speech) to assist in recall. For example, instead of trying to rote learn the eight letters in "spelling," the student can focus on the three phonemes sp-ell-ing.

- Use nonsense words to give extra practice at detecting sounds in words.

- Do not teach spelling in theme groups such as words to do with the circus. There is not enough consistency in the spelling patterns for students with dyslexia who have phonological difficulties.

- Teach spelling rules that can be applied to help with accurate spelling.

- Constantly revisit previously taught phonic families to consolidate recall.

- Constantly revisit previously taught spelling rules to consolidate recall.

Action plans for successful learning of irregular words

- Use rainbow writing. Write a word in large clear print and have the student write over it time and time again with different colored pencils to reinforce the correct spelling pattern.

- Target only a few words at a time. Write the words clearly on a note or index card. Place the card in a prominent place. Then have a fun challenge to see if the student can always spell the target words correctly. Provide reinforcements for correct spelling (such as a jelly bean each time the target word is used and written correctly).

- Make a desk dictionary. Use a large index card to list words in alphabetical order that the student uses frequently but has difficulty spelling. The card can include interesting personal words and phrases to support more risk-taking in writing.

- Have the student make a small personal dictionary (address books are good to use) to make a personal word list.

- Give multisensory practice. Encourage the student to say the letters as they are written down. Physically writing or typing a word is an important way of learning how to spell irregular words. With practice the student creates a motor memory of how to write a particular word.

- Use the *Look-Copy-Cover-Write-Check* routine to practice irregular words.

  Look: Look at the word and notice the pattern of letters. Close your eyes and try to remember how the word looks. Find groups of letters that go together.
  Copy: Copy the word down. Say the letters to yourself as you write.
  Cover: Cover the word and try to remember what it looks like.
  Write: Write the word. Say the letters to yourself as you write.
  Check: Check your spelling. If it is wrong, write it correctly. Highlight where it was wrong before and then go through the *Look-Copy-Cover-Write-Check* routine again.

- Get the student to write the word with finger painting.

- If students are learning cursive writing and need to practice, use spelling words for writing practice to double the benefits (spelling practice and handwriting practice).

- If students already write in cursive, encourage practice with weekly spelling words in cursive rather than printing (cursive writing provides a more integrated motor memory than printing).

- Make designs incorporating the correct spelling as part of the graphics.

- Practice spelling the word correctly in context. Dictate a series of short sentences, all of which contain the target word. To begin, provide a visual sample of the target word so that the student is able to refer to the model. Subsequent practice sessions should include a new set of dictation sentences containing the target word. The subsequent practice sessions should not include the visual model.

- Teach old way, new way. Analyze the way the student spells the word and teach the difference. (In the old way you used "h," in the new way you leave the "h" out.

- Use memory aids such as "we went" for the word went or "ants running everywhere" as an acronym for the word "are."

- Use the following mastery-based learning approach.

Step 1

Choose 3 or 4 words which are suitable for the student. Be sure that the student is able to read the words, understands the meaning, and is likely to use them frequently. Words that are never used by the student will not be retained beyond the teaching/testing phase.

Alternatively, test through a basic sight vocabulary list until you find three or four words that the student cannot spell. Use these as your starting point.

Step 2

On a set of small index cards, write the words you have chosen for your spelling program (one word per card). Each time the student spells the word correctly, place a tally mark on the reverse side of the card.

You will also need three separate containers to keep the cards. Label the containers: "workshop," "store," and "deposit."

Step 3

Pre-test the words which you intend to teach. Put any words that the student already knows in the "store" container.

Put words which are not yet known in the "workshop" container.

Step 4

Teach and review the words in the "workshop" container until the student is able to spell them correctly during three consecutive teaching sessions. Put a small mark on the back of the card each session to keep track of how many times the student has been able to spell it. When there are three marks on the back of the card, put it in the "store" container.

Step 5

Move on to the next list of words. Be sure to choose a suitable number, so the student is not overwhelmed with a large number of words. Go through the same process again, allocating the new words to the "workshop" or "store."

Step 6

Start each new session by revisiting the "workshop" and the "store" containers. Mark each card to show that it was recalled correctly. When six tally marks have accumulated, the words can be moved from "store" into the "deposit" container.

Step 7

Continue working on new words, introducing the words through the "workshop" container. The word is moved from "workshop" to "store" once it has three tally marks.

Step 8

About once a week, review the "deposit" container. Any words which have been forgotten go back into the "workshop" container. Once the word has three new tally marks, it moves to the "store" container. Continue marking each time the student is able to spell the word.

Step 9

Once a card has nine marks on it, it can be discarded. The student may enjoy tearing the word card up or crossing the word off a list to show it has been mastered.

Note: If the student seems to be mastering lists of words quickly, increase the number of words in each new list. If the student is finding it difficult to master the words, introduce the new words more slowly.

While nine correct attempts are usually enough to show that the words have been mastered, some students, particularly those with learning difficulties, may need additional practice. If this is the case, the number of marks at each stage may be increased before the card moves to the next level.

WRITTEN LANGUAGE

Many students with dyslexia have subtle language difficulties. They may have difficulties at the word level (poor pronunciation), or they may have difficulties at the sentence level (poor structure and organization of their sentences). In some cases, bright students may appear to be less capable than they really are because of expressive language difficulties.

One day there was a cleaner cleaning in stead of cleaning he was looking what the sciences were doing on some work the moter.

This ten year old student has an IQ of 140.

Action plans for successful learning

- Any student with a problem in the structure of either spoken or written language should be seen by a speech pathologist with expertise in language or dyslexia disorders.

- Write sentences onto strips and then cut the sentences into individual words. For older students the cards may be cut into phrases. The cards are then arranged to create the previous sentence or to make new sentences. Younger students should work with short, simple sentence construction. Older students work with complex sentences.

- Provide the student with a sentence which has a missing word. Then ask the student to fix the sentence by inserting an appropriate word.

- Provide the student with a paragraph that has a missing sentence. Then ask the student to repair the paragraph by inserting an appropriate sentence.

- Give the student sentences that have to be arranged into a logical sequence.

- Present words and phrases that have to be included in a sentence (for example, then he went, but, after all, because).

- Offer cartoon strip pictures to prompt the story line in sequence.

- Provide a picture (or series of pictures) with useful vocabulary alongside, to provide a framework for writing.

- Supply the student with a list of prompt words that help improve written expression (for example, even though, meanwhile).

- Teach planning skills using mind maps, charts, and diagrams.

- Use a suitable software program to organize ideas for written work.

- Some students find it easier to visualize a piece of written work. A story board will help turn ideas into written work.

- Give additional scaffolding (such as subheadings) to assist in the structure of a big piece of work.

- Look at how the experts do it. Take a magazine or newspaper article of interest to the student and discuss how the piece is structured. How does the author introduce the topic? What would an outline of the article look like?

- Read stories to the students to improve their awareness of sentence structure and story structure.

- Read stories and ask students to fill in the missing word when you pause. This can also give the adult insight into a student's difficulties with language.

- Allow a verbally fluent student to dictate ideas to a peer or another adult to transcribe.

- A verbally fluent student who has difficulty getting ideas down on paper might use an audio tape to record ideas. The student may later transcribe the material from the tape.

- A verbally fluent student who has difficulty getting ideas down on paper may use voice recognition software.

- Provide formal, explicit instruction in written grammar. There are numerous activity books and textbooks available for individual and classroom use.

- Use workbooks intended for students of English as a second language to provide useful additional practice in written expression.

- Older students can use predictive software on their computer. This software predicts the next word in a sentence as the students type.

- Older students also benefit from using software which can turn text into speech. The software program will allow the students to actually hear what they have written. This often helps correct poor written sentence structure.

- Older students may need additional editorial support to polish their written drafts.

- Check the setting of the grammar check on the computer that the student uses to ensure that it is set for an appropriate writing style.

- Provide simple dictation to improve the link between language and writing. Dictate the text in phrases to help the student to move from word-by-word writing to grammatically correct fluency in writing.

- Give a question plus about eight statements that are factually true and relate to the topic. Ask the student to set aside the statements which do not relate to the question being asked, even though the statements are correct.

PROOFREADING

Students with dyslexia often have significant difficulties with proofreading. The student may have no way of telling whether words are right or wrong. The student often picks correct words as errors and then rewrites them, often overlooking genuine errors.

Using a dictionary is of little help. The student may spend a lot of time looking up words that are correct and fail to check words that are wrong. Because the student is unsure of how to spell words, it is often difficult to find the word needed in the dictionary.

dangrous

It is dangerous to dive into a swimming pool because
if you don't now the depth, you may injure
youre skull, or spine when you hit the bottem.

Example of a dyslexic's proofreading. Notice how she has 'corrected' words that were right and ignored errors.

Action plans for successful learning

• Encourage the use of an adult to function as an editor or proofreader.

• Allow work to be produced on a word processor with a spellchecker and grammar checker.

• Investigate advanced software options for enhanced accuracy (for example, predictive word processing).

• Encourage the student to classify the type of error that the student usually makes (for example, a constant error such as *aer* for *are*, incorrect word endings, etc. This makes proofreading a little easier.

• Allow extra time in tests and examinations for proofreading.

• Do not penalize spelling errors unless accurate spelling is a key requirement of the task.

• Do not expect students to use a dictionary to check words. Students often think that the correct spelling is wrong and use valuable time searching the dictionary, only to find they were right all along. Students will not check words that they believe are correct. Looking up words in a dictionary is very difficult when you do not know how to spell the word.

• Use a computer program that can read back what the student has written, to assist in proofreading.

COPYING

Students with dyslexia often have great difficulties in copying things accurately. Students may copy their spelling words from the board and have errors before they even start to learn. This may mean that they do not copy homework assignments accurately and arrive home without a clear understanding of what is supposed to be done.

As well as being inaccurate, copying can also take a very long time. The student may have serious trouble in keeping up with the rest of the class.

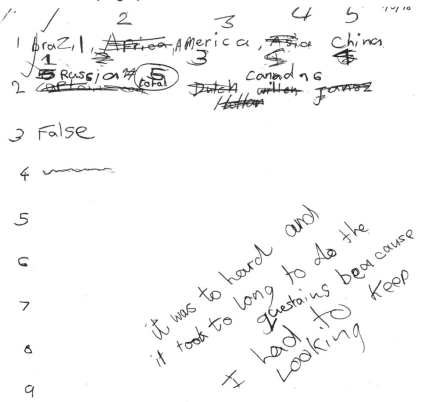

Notice how much better this student's writing is when he is writing his own words and not trying to copy from the board.

The student with dyslexia will often only recall one or two letters at a time. The student writes down two letters, looks back to the board and writes down the next one or two letters, and repeats the process over and over again. This is a slow and very frustrating process. If the student has to turn around to copy from the board, the process becomes even more difficult.

Older students can find it very difficult to access curriculum materials if they have to be copied. It is especially difficult if the teacher talks while the students are copying.

Students with dyslexia are also inaccurate at copying because they have a limited repertoire of words that they can spell. Whereas students who can spell most of the words they are copying can easily read two or three words and then write them down from memory (with correct spelling, because they already know how to spell the words), the student with dyslexia cannot do this.

Action plans for successful learning

- Avoid unnecessary copying.

- If copying is essential, ensure the student is facing the board and has an unobstructed view of the print.

- Provide worksheets rather than having students copy questions from the board or the textbook.

- Provide handouts, photocopies of notes, and printed information sheets.

- Ask a fellow student to use a carbon and create a copy for the student.

- Allow the student to photocopy or scan a fellow student's notes.

- Put essential information on a website or computer network.

- Allow extra time or shorten the task when copying is essential.

- Teach the student to divide words into manageable and meaningful subsections so that accurate copying is easier.

- When a student must copy material, check for the accuracy of what is recorded.

- In tests and exams where accurate copying is required, such as math, allow extra time.

HANDWRITING AND BOOKWORK

All young students, of course, have to acquire the basic skills of writing as they start school. For some students this process is quick and easy, but for many students with dyslexia, the process is slow and tedious.

Before students can actually learn how to form letters, they must be able not only to control a pencil but also to understand how to form various shapes. For instance, the student must be able to create a smooth curve (necessary for letters such as o and c), combined straight lines and curves (n, m, u, b), and diagonal lines (y, x, v, w).

Capital letters are easier than lower case letters because they are formed from less complex shapes (more straight lines and fewer complex mixes of curves and straight lines). However, it is important that younger students are introduced to lower case rather than upper case, particularly if they are likely to have problems with writing. Some students use a mixture of upper and lower case letters. This may sometimes be to avoid letter reversals or may be due to poor awareness of the difference between the two types of letters and their respective uses.

While some writing difficulties are due to muscle problems, most are caused by motor-planning problems. Unfortunately, while muscle problems very often improve quickly and easily with training, motor-planning problems (caused by a dysfunction in the neurological pathway between the brain and the hand) are much less easily treated.

Although students do improve with practice, there are some students who have ongoing and significant difficulties with handwriting despite expert therapy and huge amounts of practice. Severe handwriting difficulties are called dysgraphia. Dysgraphia is a recognized disability, and students with dysgraphia are usually eligible for special provisions when they take examinations.

The advice "Try harder-do better" can cause substantial frustration to the dyslexic student whose best efforts produce an illegible scrawl.

Students with dyslexia often have difficulty with sustained handwriting. The student can write very neatly for a short while, but after that the handwriting deteriorates very rapidly. In a classroom situation, this may mean that the student is able to write for a little while and then must stop to rest the hand. This may look as if the student is inattentive or distracted. Sometimes a student's difficulties with sustained writing do not become evident until students start to take examinations. Writing for two to three hours can be an impossible challenge for some students who have previously managed to get by writing in bursts of five or ten minutes.

Taking notes in class can be very demanding for the student who has difficulty with sustained writing. Notes may be incomplete or illegible.

Word processing is often less neurologically challenging than handwriting. It is much less likely that there will be problems with sustained writing using a keyboard. However, some students find that typing is just as difficult as handwriting.

Students with dyslexia often have to make a choice between speed and neatness. They can produce neat work, provided they work extremely carefully and slowly and take rest breaks. This, of course, is not an efficient way of producing work. When asked to rewrite untidy work, the student may struggle even to match the neatness of the first draft.

Students often realize that it is easier to produce a short neat piece of work (with no rewrites) than to produce a lengthy, interesting, but untidy piece of work (when a tedious rewrite is certain to be required).

Many students have extreme difficulty with neatness. They may have memory difficulties and be poor at copying. The student may have to constantly look backwards and forwards between book and board. This in itself makes the letters irregular and poorly spaced because they are written one at a time and not fluently as a whole word.

Many youngsters have problems with the spatial/perceptual aspects of bookwork such as being able to organize print neatly on a page, space words evenly, and write letters neatly. Some students have trouble judging how much space is needed for a particular word, so that they are constantly running out of space at the end of a line. Others may overcompensate and stop in the middle of the page to make sure they have room for the next word, which they often write on the next line.

Poor bookwork can cause enormous frustration to adults and students alike. This is particularly so when there is a high emphasis on neatness. Students need to be reassured that neatness is not, in itself, a critical academic attribute.

Action plans for successful learning

- Beginning writers should write with lower case letters. Parents of preschoolers should be reminded of this if they plan to teach their child to write.

- Provide tactile experience with letter formation. Spread icing, sugar, shaving foam, pudding, or any other tactile material on a flat surface and allow the students to trace the letter shapes with their fingertips. The adult may need to place a hand over the student's for guidance.

- Experiment to find the best type of writing tool. Soft lead pencils, roller ball style pens, or fine tip markers may give a smoother line and make writing easier and clearer.

- Seat a left-handed writer to the left of a right-handed writer to avoid collisions.

- Minimize unnecessary writing. Provide worksheets, printed handouts, or photocopies rather than requiring the student to take notes.

- Accept that writing which is neat will not be quick.

- Emphasize that quality of the content counts for much more than neatness.

- Accept that the student may well produce work which is messy and untidy, even with the best effort.

- Accept that neatness will deteriorate rapidly when volume or speed is required.

- Make it clear to the student whether neatness or speed is required. Accept that the student may not be able to produce both neatness and speed simultaneously.

- Encourage the development of good word-processing skills. Rough drafts can be typed up, printed out, edited, and reprinted.

- Assess the student with oral rather than written tests.

- Negotiate extra time in examinations for the student with writing difficulties.

- Negotiate for the student to use a word processor instead of handwriting in examinations.

- Allow for rest breaks when the student has a lot of writing to do.

- Use a peer or another adult to transcribe and support the student with handwriting and typing difficulties.

- Use voice recognition software for the student who has both writing and typing difficulties.

- If possible, do not require the student to rewrite messy work if it is legible.

- Provide someone to type the work if the content is good but presentation poor.

- Write on alternate lines to allow space for corrections.

- Provide alternate forms of paper (pages with preprinted borders, interesting colored paper, etc.) so the final presentation is not dependent on the student's ability to be neat and tidy.

- Grade separately for content and neatness. Give content a high percentage of the overall grade and neatness a much smaller percentage.

- Give short tasks that the student can complete in the time available, to teach the student the skill of seeing a task through to completion.

- Provide appropriate seating arrangements. If a small child must use an adult-sized table, provide a box for the feet and a cushion for the back so the student has firm support.

- In school, be sure the table and chair are the correct height for the student and that they adopt a good writing posture (chair tucked in, feet firmly on the floor, back against the chair).

- Allow shortcuts such as photocopying text and adding notes.

LETTER AND NUMBER REVERSALS

Many young students reverse letters and numerals. Some students may continue reversing letters beyond the age of seven, and maybe even to adulthood.

The problem in reversing letters and numerals is often caused by an error in the neurological pathway which triggers the hand to make the letter movement. While memory aids such as "The bat comes before the ball" can help, often they add to confusion for the student. This mnemonic depends on the student knowing before means to the left of the letter and knowing left from right.

A more effective strategy is to use an existing neurological pathway that is already established for another letter.

Action plans for successful learning

- Teach **b** as an extension of the letter **h** (using the same neurological pathway). Start off with the **h** and continue the stroke around to form the **b**. The memory prompt for this can be hubba bubba.

h b h b h b h b

- Teach **d** by using the existing neurological pathway for **a**. Start off with the letter **a** and continue the vertical stroke upwards. The memory prompt for this could be dad or add.

a d a d a d a d

- The letter **p** is based on the neurological pathway for the letter **n**. The vertical stroke is extended downwards and the curve is completed. The memory prompt for this could be nipper.

n p n p n p n p

- Give tactile experience of letter and numeral formation. Spread icing, sugar, shaving foam, or any other tactile material on a flat surface, and get the student to trace the letter or numeral shape with the fingertip.

Chapter 5

MATHEMATICS

MULTIPLICATION TABLES

THE LANGUAGE OF MATH

SPATIAL AWARENESS AND MATH

MULTIPLICATION TABLES

One of the primary disorders in dyslexia is difficulty in remembering sequenced information, such as multiplication tables.

Multiplication tables are challenging because they require good memory of basic number facts and also require the student to remember the sequence of individual items in the multiplication table. Many students get lost when they are reciting their tables. They lose their place, skip items, or go back and repeat some items over again.

Students with dyslexia may be paradoxical math students, finding the easy arithmetic difficult, but conceptually challenging math relatively straightforward. Difficulties in learning tables can cause considerable frustration, particularly if there is emphasis in the classroom on quick, accurate recall of multiplication tables. Even very bright students may find this one of the hardest things of all to master. Other sequences which students may have difficulties with include days of the week, months of the year, and sequences of words or sounds (spelling, telephone numbers, or their own date of birth).

Action plans for successful learning

- Provide a calculator or number square when teaching a new math process. This will help to avoid memory difficulties from interfering with new learning.

- Do not estimate a student's math potential by only assessing arithmetic (recall of number facts, mental manipulation of numbers).

- Accept that inconsistency in recall of rote learned information is a common trait of students with learning disabilities.

- Give the student a sheet with the tables written on it (with answers missing) so as they recite their tables, they do not lose their place.

- Show students how, once they have learned one or two multiplication tables, additional parts of the other tables have been mastered.

- Use number grids to provide multiplication table practice. This is often much easier than reciting a table all through.

- Prepare a sequence of number grids of increasing challenge. Use a ten-by-ten square for all the grids and blank out the items not yet introduced.

Levels of difficulty for time tables grids:

Level 1:   1x,   2x
Level 2:   1x,   2x,   3x
Level 3:   1x,   2x,   3x,   4x
Level 4:   1x,   2x,   3x,   4x,   5x
Level 5:   1x,   2x,   3x,   4x,   5x,   6x
Level 6:   1x,   2x,   3x,   4x,   5x,   6x,   7x
Level 7:   1x,   2x,   3x,   4x,   5x,   6x,   7x,   8x
Level 8:   1x,   2x,   3x,   4x,   5x,   6x,   7x,   8x,   9x
Level 9:   1x,   2x,   3x,   4x,   5x,   6x,   7x,   8x,   9x,   10x

Sample of Level 4 number grid:

The sample below is for the Level 4 number grid. The student practices the multiplication facts for 1x, 2x, 3x, 5x, and 10x at this time. The shaded areas will be practiced at another level.

	1	2	3	4	5	6	7	8	9	10
1										
2										
3										
4										
5										
6										
7										
8										
9										
10										

- For students who have mastered 50% or more of their tables, introduce speed and accuracy drills to consolidate what they already know. Gradually build in the remaining tables as the student gains confidence and speed.

- For students who are ten years and over who know less than 50% of their tables, accept that the effort and frustration involved in learning tables may not justify the outcome. Encourage the student to use a calculator or number chart instead.

- When learning tables, remember that over-learning is essential for the student with dyslexia. This means that the student may need to go over the same facts time and time again and must also constantly review the facts to prevent them being lost.

THE LANGUAGE OF MATH

Many dyslexic students have difficulties with the language of math. The student may understand the concepts but get muddled up with the language. Language which relates to direction of operations may be particularly difficult. For example, understanding the difference between phrases such as *Take six from nine* and *Take nine from six* may be very difficult. Other mathematical terms such as *divided by, shared into, half of, twice as much,* and *equals* can be very confusing for a dyslexic student.

Word problems may also be challenging for a student who has problems with interpreting complex language.

> A difficult question for a dyslexic student with subtle language difficulties:
>
> Question: *If you have three marbles in each hand, how many marbles do you have altogether?*
> Answer: *But I haven't got three hands.*

Students with word-finding difficulties may have difficulties producing the right answer quickly when put on the spot.

Students with reading difficulties may also have problems reading worksheets and other curriculum materials.

Action plans for successful learning

- Provide a language-rich mathematical environment where the language of math is used in an everyday context. Use play, travel, construction, cooking, gardening, games, sports, and creative activities to promote the use of math and the language of math in a real life setting.

- Check that the student really understands basic mathematical language such as more than, less than, greater, shared, middle, etc., when teaching new concepts.

- Use consistent terminology when first introducing a new concept. For example do not interchange between minus, subtract, and take away when first introducing subtraction.

- Think aloud to give the student insight into the internal language that accompanies the process that you are teaching. For example, when teaching the steps to addition say: "I've got to add 3 to 5. So I'll get three blocks and then I'll get five blocks. Now I will put them all in a line and count them to see how many I have altogether. Now I can write the number here." This helps the student with language difficulties to understand how other people think things through using internal language.

- Provide training sessions and information sheets for parents so that they can use the same methods and the same language at home as is being used in the classroom.

- Provide the older student with a glossary of mathematical words and phrases with worked examples where needed.

- Provide reality-based alternatives to explain math terminology. For example, refer to groups of instead of multiply so that the student can read 3 x 2 as three groups of two.

- Practice matching number sentences (8+5, 12-6, 5x4, etc.) to real actions with concrete materials such as plastic toys, animals, cubes, etc., (real items work better than counters). Place some toy animals and an index card with the problem 5 x 4 on the desk, and then say "Show me 5 x 4 with the animals."

- Show the student how to find key words in written word problems which provide a clue to the process required. "Altogether" usually indicates an addition or multiplication problem. "How many were left?" is a subtraction problem.

- When word problems are being given, encourage the student to draw a simple sketch of the problem. This will help the student to visualize the problem in pictures, not words.

- Provide a reading buddy to support the student in reading math worksheets.

- Write mental arithmetic questions for the student who has language processing or memory difficulties.

- Allow the student with a language-fluency or word-finding problem to write the multiplication tables rather than verbalize them.

- Look for a pattern of errors in the student's work. This will help to diagnose whether the errors occur in the process or the calculation.

- Ask the student to think aloud while working so that you can hear the language and method being used.

Sam was having a lot of trouble with his early math. He was asked to show his teacher what he did.

He looked at the sheet of numbers and then looked away, half closed his eyes, and touch-counted his fingers. Then he wrote a number down. Asked what he had just done, he said:

"I counted like Sarah does."

Sam was just copying Sarah's behavior and did not understand the internal language that was taking place when Sarah worked out the answer! Because he was only working with numbers less than ten, he sometimes got the correct answer just by chance.

SPATIAL AWARENESS AND MATH

Some students with dyslexia have considerable difficulty with spatial awareness.

Understanding concepts that rely on an awareness of patterning can be difficult for the student. These difficulties range from tangible problems with shape and form to more abstract difficulties in understanding order of magnitude (is 46 larger or small than 53?), relative position of numerals (is it 13 or 31?), or a mathematical situation (If pencils costs $1.50 a box, how many boxes can I buy if I have $9 to spend?)

Teaching fractions is often done with diagrams. Unfortunately, diagrams may confuse rather than help the student with spatial awareness difficulties.

Understanding clock faces can be another major challenge for the student with spatial difficulties.

Another significant problem for the student with spatial-awareness difficulties is with directionality. Young students usually begin their work horizontally, working from left to right (the same direction as printed language), rather than vertically.

However, soon the math problems are arranged vertically and worked from right to left. This change of direction and sequence of actions can be very confusing.

52	15	16	13
+35	+23	+71	+99
87	65	87	184

24	28	35	36
+32	+81	+53	+62
56	109	88	98

This student's working method was to add the top two figures together and record the total. She also added the bottom two numbers together and recorded that total. She was inconsistent in the order in which she did this and in where she positioned her totals. In most of these examples, she got the right answer with the wrong method!

Once regrouping and exchanging is introduced, the student has to work from right to left but also has to remember to work from the top to the bottom and sometimes has to record diagonally (depending on the methods being taught).

Students can find tasks such as copying numbers accurately, lining up columns of figures, and writing numbers accurately very challenging.

Drawing geometric shapes and geometric reasoning may also be a challenge for the student. Students with spatial-awareness difficulties often look as if they have a coordination problem when, in fact, they have reasonable physical control over their pencil, but run into difficulties in interpreting and reproducing complex spatial forms.

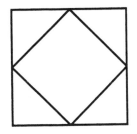

This is a dyslexic's copy of a spatial form

Action plans for successful learning

- Give explicit teaching when teaching math calculations.

- Provide visual prompts such as a green margin on the right hand side of the page to help the student remember which side to start working from.

- Provide printed worksheets so the student may work the problem and provide the answer on the worksheet in place of copying the entire problem.

- Provide a "recipe book" of step-by-step instructions and examples for each process.

- Provide the student with graph paper if copying is required.

- Try using lined paper placed on its side to provide vertical columns.

- Provide a calculator with a printout so students can show their work, despite problems with neatness.

- Teach how to write the numbers 13 to 19 with the memory prompt: "You have to be one before you are thirteen," etc.

- Teach reading the clock face in five separate stages:

Teach the student to tell the time using only the hour hand. This will obviously be an approximation. Say: "It's nearly half past six," "it's nearly eight o'clock," etc.

Teach the student to read the minute hand: quarter past, half past, quarter to, etc. Team this with the information from the hour hand.

Teach the student to read the minutes 1-30: twenty past, five past, etc. Team this with the hour hand: twenty past six, five past four, etc.

Teach the student to read the minutes 31-60 as twenty to, five to (the mirror image of stage three when they read twenty past), etc. Team this with the hour hand: ten to six, twenty to three, etc.

Teach the equivalence of "past" and "to". Ten to six is the same as fifty minutes past five.

- Teach fractions with language.

  If we cut a cake into six equal pieces, each piece is called a sixth. If we cut a cake into five equal pieces, each piece will be called a...?

  If we cut a cake into eight equal pieces, each piece will be called a ...? If we have two pieces of the cake, we have two ...? If we have three pieces of the cake, we have...?

  We write it down like this. We put the number 8 at the bottom. This number tells us how many pieces the cake was cut into. Now we put a 3 on the top. This number tells us how many pieces of cake we have.

  Look at this: 5/8. How many pieces of cake are there? Look at the bottom number. How many of those pieces do we have? Look at the top number.

.

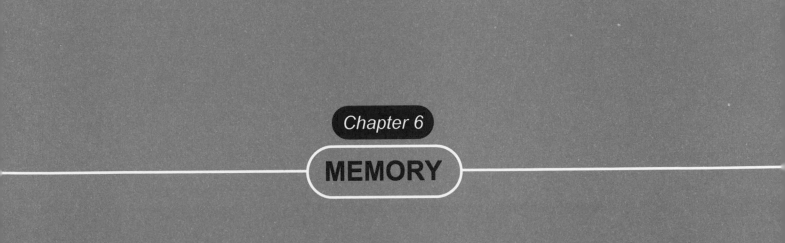

Chapter 6

MEMORY

MEMORY AND DYSLEXIA

MEMORY AND DYSLEXIA

Students with dyslexia frequently have difficulties with short-term memory. Typically, they will have difficulty in retaining sequenced information such as multiple instructions, days of the week, multiplication tables, and the sequence of letters in spelling.

The student's long-term memory is often very good. Long-term memory often depends on understanding, not parrot-fashion learning. Students may find it very difficult to remember how to spell a word from one day to the next, but have no trouble at all in remembering in detail a visit they made several years ago.

The student will often remember best when given information in more than one modality.

Often, the student does not use internal rehearsal (saying something over and over in the mind) to help to retain information.

Students often find it difficult to "sift out" what they have to listen to and what they can safely ignore.

The mechanism of memory is complex, and irregularities can occur in processing, storage, or retrieval of information. There are two important types of memory that underpin successful learning:

Listening (auditory) memory is needed to remember instructions and information, and to help process letter sounds when reading and spelling. Auditory memory also supports recitation learning such as multiplication tables.

Visual (eidetic) memory helps to store the appearance of words for reading, spelling, copying, and proofreading.

There are various factors that make memory difficulties much more pronounced.

Concentration difficulties: For short-term memory to work, we need to be able to concentrate on what we are trying to remember. Many students are easily distracted and, therefore do not take in what is being said.

However, poor short-term memory in itself can mimic poor concentration. Students with dyslexia may listen carefully but forget what has just been said. Diagnostically, it is often difficult to tell what is happening in this chicken-and-egg situation. However, the combined impact of poor short-term memory and difficulties with concentration is often a major source of frustration for students and their teachers alike.

Anxiety: Memory is very vulnerable to disruption by anxiety. The physical consequences of anxiety (dry mouth, faster heart rate, etc.) and the cognitive consequences of anxiety (agitation, preoccupation, and distraction) make it significantly harder for short-term memory to function properly.

Expectation of failure: We know that expectation of failure often generates self talk, where the internal monologue of the student runs along the lines of "Oh, I'll never, ever remember this.", "This is so hard.", "I'm going to be in big trouble if I don't learn this quickly." This type of thinking disrupts the memory process. The information which the student is trying to learn is pushed to one side by the negative internal speech which goes along with expecting failure.

Fatigue: None of us finds it as easy to learn things if we are tired. Students with dyslexia are often very tired, because they have to work so hard during each school day simply to keep their head above water. This in itself will make rote learning more difficult for them, especially late in the day when the student is usually expected to complete homework.

Having too much to remember at once: Students often become overloaded with what they have to learn. Because they have difficulties with memory, each piece of learning takes more time and effort. This means, of course, that they cannot cope with the same volume of material as other students.

Not having the opportunity to consolidate learning: We know that learning is most successful if a period of intense input is followed by a quiet time where the information can "sink in" and consolidate. If a student has to learn new material without sufficient time for reflection and consolidation, then new learning will push out earlier learning before it has had time to be properly established in the memory.

Action plans for successful learning

- Teach memory strategies. Brainstorm with the class to find out how other students remember things. Talk about mental rehearsal, organizing ideas, recording, and planning.

- Have the students ask their family members about how they remember things.

- Ask the student to activate memory strategies: "How are you going to remember this? What will be the best way for you to learn this?"

- Teach the student to use recall memory when studying. Rereading notes activates recognition memory but does not help with recall. Use mini-tests, draw diagrams, and rewrite from memory to activate recall.

- Give memory based work at a time of day when the student is not tired.

- Break large memory tasks into a series of small tasks

- Make a clear distinction between definite requirements and optional activities. Students with memory difficulties may not even attempt to remember apparent nonessentials such as, "I would like you to ask at home for some old magazines."

- Be explicit when things have to be remembered, and try to activate the student's memory strategies. "This is priority 1. Everyone needs to bring in their field trip permission slip by tomorrow at nine o'clock. Everyone stop right now and think about how you are going to remember this. Jack, what's your plan for remembering your slip?"

- Engage the student's interest by using the analogy of saving a document on a computer. "Save this information on your hard drive. Say it over to yourself to get it to save. Save it in your 'must do tomorrow' file. Open the file up to check it is saved properly. Print it out and put the print out in your bag."

- Make sure the student has time for rest and relaxation to allow fragile learning to consolidate.

- Provide memory prompts such as dot points on the board to summarize instructions. Provide a written checklist of daily routine.

- Make sure that the student feels confident and relaxed to optimize recall.

- Avoid making scores from memory tests public knowledge, as this increases anxiety and reduces recall.

- Avoid creating time pressure when recall is needed. Let the students work on their own time frame.

- Allow a scribble pad to be used in mental arithmetic tests.

- Let the students say when they are ready to be assessed so they can allow enough time to prepare, which will help to reduce anxiety.

- Give mental arithmetic and spelling tests one-on-one if possible. The adult can pace the questions to suit the student.

- Allow plenty of time for rote learning.

- Encourage students to use mnemonics (memory prompts) to help with recall. Ones they make up themselves often work best.

- Encourage the student to make notes to compensate for poor memory.

- Encourage students to ask for information to be repeated if they have forgotten it.

- Prioritize what must be learned so that the student does not expend valuable time and energy on low priority memory work.

- Keep instructions short and clear. Long strings of instructions may need to be broken up so that only one instruction is given at a time. The student follows through the first instruction, and then the next instruction is given.

- Emphasize the sequence of the instructions: "First finish your worksheet, then tidy your desk and then you can get on with your poster."

- Instead of just verbally giving instructions, give a demonstration, draw a diagram or picture, or use a tangible way of showing what to do. Pin up a worksheet, put the waste bin on display, hold up a partly completed poster, etc.

- Tell the students the number of things they need to remember. "There are three important things you need to remember. Number one, you must start with a clean page. Number two, write in pencil. Number three, copy the date from the board. Remember, three things: clean page, pencil, and date."

- Get the students to monitor the number of things they have completed. "You have to do four things. Number one, you need to brush your teeth. Number two, you have to put your clothes in the basket. Number three, you have to feed the dog. Number four, you need to put your lunchbox in your bag."

Here are your four marbles. Put one in the jar each time you have finished a job.
I want to see four marbles in the jar by the time I've finished washing the dishes.

- Use checklists or tangible reminders for the students to physically monitor what they have to do. Items are crossed off the checklist and tangible reminders (such as adhesive notes) are discarded once the task has been done.

- Provided the student is able to read sufficiently well, back up any verbal information in written form, such as dot points on the board or a printed list of instructions to take home.

- It is important that you have the student's attention before you give important information. "Everyone stop what they are doing and listen carefully."

- Signal when you are about to give out important information. Try to make it interesting to catch the students' interest. "News Flash! We have just heard from our reporter in the front office that the dates for the field trip have been determined."

- Vary the way classroom instructions and other information are given. Get a student to read out loud what is required, draw the instructions, mime from your written list, or give it in rap form.

- Give the student a reason for listening carefully: "This is a short cut for your homework."

- Impose a thinking time after an instruction has been given: "Everyone take a minute to think over what I have just said. Then repeat the information once more."

- Impose thinking time to encourage recall of previous instructions. "It is Thursday tomorrow, so stop and think what is special about Thursday. Before we go home, let's take one minute's thinking time. Think through everything you need to have in your bag for tonight's homework."

- Encourage repetition of what has just been said. "Just let me check that I told you all the details; tell me what you have to do."

- Many students who have memory problems also have concentration and organization difficulties. The next chapter on Concentration includes many more ideas.

Chapter 7

CONCENTRATION

QUIET INATTENTIVENESS

DISTRACTIBILITY AND IMPULSIVENESS

PHYSICAL RESTLESSNESS

POOR ORGANIZATION

CONCENTRATION

Characteristics such as poor auditory processing can easily mimic concentration difficulties.

Any student (dyslexic or not) can have medical problems such as sleep disorders, minor forms of epilepsy, fatigue, etc., which can impair the student's ability to remain focused. Many students with concentration difficulties also have problems with memory (see Chapter 5).

Some youngsters seem inattentive and poorly motivated because they are anxious, are depressed, or have other emotional difficulties or social problems.

Very bright students may also be suspected of having poor concentration because they are bored, even though they are finding the basic chore of learning difficult.

Many students also have concentration difficulties (ranging from mild to severe), and some may be diagnosed as having Attention Deficit Disorder (with or without hyperactivity). This means that you may be working with a student who has not one but two disabilities (dyslexia and ADD).

Good management is always the first priority in addressing the needs of the student with concentration problems.

A cognitive behavioral approach is the core of a good management program for concentration difficulties. This means students are helped to become aware of their own concentration style and to shape their own behavior through awareness, planning, and self monitoring.

Adult understanding, positive encouragement, and patience are also crucial in successfully managing concentration difficulties.

Medication can sometimes have a role to play, particularly when the student's concentration difficulties are so severe that even with careful, positive management, their inattentiveness still interferes with their learning.

QUIET INATTENTIVENESS

Some students sit quietly "in a world of their own." Often they are very slow at completing assignments and are forgetful and disorganized. Because of inattentiveness, the student needs frequent reminders to get started and stay on track. They may waste time getting started or take too much time on minor elements of the assignment, such as coloring the title page instead of writing the story.

Action plans for successful learning

- Refer the student to an appropriate specialist (pediatrician, psychologist, or neurologist) for a medical assessment if the student's inattentiveness causes severe problems in school.

- Check the level and pace of the schoolwork to be sure it is at the appropriate level for the student. Consider the possibility that the student might be bright/bored and dyslexic.

- Ask questions so that the students begin to understand the problem for themselves. *I didn't get started quickly enough so I haven't finished yet. I think I was daydreaming instead of getting the task done. I spent too much time on the fiddly bits and ran out of time for the important part of the task. I didn't have the right equipment on my desk.*

- Involve the student in planning ways to help overcome the problems of inattentiveness. *I can ask my friend or my teacher to remind me to concentrate. I can start on the most important part first. I can get started right away. I can get ready in good time. I can write a note to myself.*

- Let students share ideas about how to stay on task. *I keep reminding myself to keep working. I keep telling myself to stay focused. I go as fast as I can. I try not to do anything else until I have finished. I set my stop watch to see how long it takes me.*

- Encourage the students to self-monitor their concentration and to let you know how they are progressing. *Today I got all my things ready for math quickly and I was nearly the first student to get started on the worksheet.*

- Ask each inattentive student to nominate a classmate as a pace maker. The student undertakes the challenge to try to equal or exceed their pace maker's work output.

- Give the student frequent, quiet reminders to stay on task.

- Provide short pieces of work and definite time limits.

- Make instruction as interesting as possible (use color, drama, music, humor, demonstrations, etc.)

- Allow extra time for work to be completed.

- Give explicit training in seeing one task through to completion without a break.

- Prioritize work so that the student gets started on the most important piece of work first.

- Use visual prompts such as gold stars to remind the student of what is important.

- Use short cuts to minimize the time taken on a piece of work.

- Have the student work against the clock or use a stopwatch.

- Play games such as Snap where vigilance and fast reactions are needed.

- Allow for some activities where a quiet, reflective approach is appropriate.

- Give the student explicit, positive feedback for attentive behavior. Give tickets. "You are working well." "You finished on time." These are placed on the student's desk as appropriate and can be traded for small rewards.

- Older students who daydream or are off-task may need a "prompter" in important examinations to be sure they stay on task.

- Use checklists to help the student remember an organization routine. For example, ask the student to place a list of the morning reminders on the bedroom mirror at home or on the desk at school. In the beginning, the student may need to be reminded to look at the list.

DISTRACTIBILITY AND IMPULSIVENESS

Many students with dyslexia are easily distracted and impulsive. Punishments and rewards do not have much effect because the student does not stop and think about consequences before they act.

Many students, with or without ADD, will make careless errors. The student will probably find copying from the board, correct spelling, and proofreading difficult, even with good concentration. Obviously, a student with both dyslexia and ADD will have a lot of trouble with neat, accurate work.

Action plans for successful learning

- Refer the student to an appropriate specialist (pediatrician, psychologist, or neurologist) for medical assessment if the student's distractibility and impulsiveness cause severe problems in school.

- Ask questions to help the students understand their own distractibility and impulsiveness. *I didn't stop and think. I forgot to read the instructions. I wasn't watching what I was doing. I answered before I had time to think.*

- Help the student to devise and implement strategies for managing impulsive, inattentive behavior. *I need to stop and think before I answer. I have to remember to read the instructions. I have to tell myself to listen carefully. I need to write it down and put it where I will remember it. I have to remind myself to concentrate.*

- Encourage the students to self-evaluate their concentration and impulse control and to tell you about their successes. *You know, when Billy was messing around, I said to myself, 'Keep working', and I did. I didn't let him distract me.*

- Ask students to share ideas about how to manage distractions. *I put all my stuff away so I don't fiddle with it. I tell myself 'don't turn around; keep your eyes and ears on the teacher.'*

- Alert students to situations where a high level of concentration is needed.

- Seat the student close to where the teacher usually stands.

- Reduce the distractions (such as mobiles, fish tanks, open doors, etc.) that are in the students' view.

- Keep the student's working area clear of distractions. Allow one small item to "fiddle with" if this helps the student to focus.

- Speak slowly and quietly to bring an impulsive student down to a quieter, more reasonable level. Impulsive students get even more agitated if adults are loud and excitable.

- Allow for a cooling-off place for an impulsive student who has "gone over the top".

- Provide an "office" (a three-sided screen) to place on the student's desk.

- Offer the student a separate desk (not as a punishment, but as a way to help minimize distractions).

- Provide plenty of opportunities to move around and "let off steam".

- Structure tasks into short, easy-to-manage sections.

- Give explicit training in seeing one task through to completion without a break.

- Use silent reminders. For example, just move closer to the student and make eye contact.

- Encourage the student to self monitor individual concentration. Give the student a rating card to tally their perception of their ability to focus at regular intervals.

- Break the school day into short sections, and give the student positive feedback for periods of positive application.

- Older students may need a "prompter" for important tests or examinations to make sure they stay on task.

- Have fun activities to practice ignoring distractions. Students are put in pairs and one of each pair has to concentrate on a simple task (such as a dot-to-dot puzzle). The other partner in the pair has to try to distract the worker without actually touching the person. Obviously, roles are then reversed, so that each student has a turn of being a "worker" and a "distracter."

- Teach the students that "fast" or "first" is not necessarily "best."

- Get students to use the "pause button" to stop and think before they begin a task.

- Distribute worksheets but ask the students to look at the worksheet for sixty seconds to determine what they have to do before they are allowed to pick up their pencils.

- Have fun "stop and think" activities. Ask the class a series of easy questions which have "yes" or "no" answers. The trick is that answers cannot be called out until five seconds has elapsed. Anyone who calls out the answer before the five seconds is out. Anyone who calls out the wrong answer after 5 seconds is also out. You can use right hand raised for "yes" and left hand raised for "no" instead.

- Give "tickets" that entitle students to have a turn speaking in group discussions. Each student receives a specific number of tickets which must be used economically. Once their tickets are used up, they cannot make any more comments. (This is also great for encouraging the less vocal children to take their turn.)

- Prepare cards with statements such as: *You are working well. You are on task. You stopped and thought. You waited your turn.* Place these cards on the student's desk as appropriate. These cards can be traded off for a small reward.

- Introduce relaxation training, yoga, tai chi, or any other activity which requires control and quiet reflection.

PHYSICAL RESTLESSNESS

Many children and adolescents are restless and fidgety. Sometimes this interferes with their learning and sometimes it does not.

The level of sensory input which each person needs (children and adults alike) varies considerably. Some people are very comfortable with a low level of sensory input. Children and adults who need a high level of sensory input will always need to be moving, touching, or fidgeting to keep their system in its comfort zone of sensory input.

Children with poor muscle tone will also seem restless and fidgety because they do not have sufficient muscle tone to maintain a steady, controlled position.

Action plans for successful learning

- Arrange appropriate medical assessment and treatment with a pediatrician or occupational therapist if restlessness seriously impacts on the student's learning.

- Check to see whether the student's restless, fidgety behavior actually interferes with learning. If it does not, then no action is needed other than to ensure that other students are not disturbed.

- Give the restless student plenty of space so that the restless, fidgety behavior does not disturb others.

- Provide something to "fiddle with," such as a squishy ball or a piece of clay, for the student who simply can't sit still.

- Sitting on the floor is extremely uncomfortable for some students with poor muscle tone. Allow the child to sit on the chair at the edge of the group instead of on the floor.

- Be sure that desk and chair is of appropriate size for the student.

- Accept that students with poor muscle tone will have difficulty sitting up straight and will tend to slouch or sprawl as they work.

POOR ORGANIZATION

Many dyslexic students have significant difficulties with organization. Sometimes this is part of their avoidance behavior, but more often it is a genuine part of their learning disorder.

What is called "executive function" (looking ahead, planning appropriately, following through, etc.) is often a significant problem for the student with dyslexia. Students often feel overwhelmed because the work is too difficult, or they have too much work to do in the time available. Many students have short-term memory difficulties or auditory processing problems, and have difficulties writing things down, so they may not have a clear idea about what they are supposed to do.

The student will often need explicit, clear directions. The poorly organized student often assumes that good organization just happens.

The emotional consequences of dyslexia can also have an impact on personal organization. Students who are depressed or anxious will find it difficult to see the big picture and often fail to be well organized.

Action plans for successful learning

- Model good organization so the student can see how it is done.

- Brainstorm at home and at school for organization tips that others use.

- Set small, achievable goals in aiming to improve organization.

- Ask to student to think about organization. *How are you going to make sure that you get all of this done by Thursday? How are you going to remember to give this note to your teacher?*

- Ensure the student is equipped with a set of working equipment (pencil, ruler, eraser, etc.) before the task is started. Have spare supplies readily available to avoid wasting time looking for an essential item.

- Get the student to keep all loose papers in one large folder or file.

- Get the student a transparent zip wallet or bag. Let the student decorate it to make it as distinctive as possible so it is harder to lose! This holds all important notices or material that has to be dealt with urgently.

- Remind the student to use the wallet or zip-lock bag. *This is important. Put it in your wallet (bag) right away.*

- At home the parents should be aware of the wallet (bag) so that it may be checked. *Do you have anything in the wallet (bag) today?*

- Negotiate with the students the ways they want adults to help them. *I'd like Mom to write a note and put it on my pillow to remind me to pack my bag.*

- Students often rely on adults reminding them over and over again. Teach the student that there will be a limited number of reminders. (Three is usually plenty!) *This is the last reminder Jess. After this you need to remember your sports gear on your own..*

- Provide structure and routine so that it is easier for good organization to become automatic.

- Ask questions rather than give orders. *Today is Tuesday. What you need to remember?* instead of *It's Tuesday, get your swimming stuff.*

- Build thinking and planning time into the schedule at home and at school. *OK now stand still for one minute and then tell me what you have to do today.*

- Adults should try to avoid constant "rescue" missions for poorly organized students. For example, if sports gear is forgotten, it stays at home.

- Being poorly organized should not mean that the student manages to avoid reasonable but unwelcome tasks.

- Give the student responsibility for organizing pleasant events such as a family outing or a family meal.

- Once the responsibility for organizational tasks has been allocated adults should not fuss or interfere.

- Clarify who will do what. *OK all planned. You are going to take responsibility for everything to do with the drinks. You will need cups, glasses, straws, ice, and drinks. Here's $10 to buy what you need. I am going to do the sandwiches and Dad is going to take care of the snacks. The drinks are your responsibility.*

- Avoid overloading with work and play activities to minimize what has to be organized.

- Where time limits are relevant, make these explicit to the student and remind the student to use a timer, alarm watch, etc., to keep track of time.

Chapter 8

MOTIVATION

WORKLOAD

MOTIVATION, CONFIDENCE, AND STRESS

ACCEPTANCE

WORKLOAD

Many students with dyslexia have to work extremely hard for very limited results. Frequently, the workload flows through to parents, who have to put in a lot of time in supporting the student. The student may have the basic class homework and unfinished work from school, plus special education homework. Some students will go to extra tutoring or therapy out of school.

MATHS: In maths am OK but am a bid blow awrich. I stugel in loning my tadel I injoy prodlem saveing and reading grichs. My log dvechen iset vere good sort drichen is eser. I have inprooved at every thing and I stagel at But I have stagel much this yare

This student has written "MATH: In math I am OK but I am a bit below average. I struggle in learning my tables. I enjoy problem solving and reading groups. My long division isn't very good short division is easier. I have improved at everything (that) I struggle at. But I have struggled much this year."

If a student with dyslexia works slowly, the student may never finish the work in the time available. This is discouraging and sets up poor work habits.

There will be some families who may spend two or three hours most weekdays helping their primary school child complete homework. Students with learning disabilities (and their families) can get very tired and discouraged by the seemingly never-ending work load.

Work that may have taken hours for the student to complete can look as if it has been rushed through in a few minutes. The combination of high effort and poor outcome is probably one of the most frustrating aspects of dyslexia.

I feel like School is a jail becase The work is to hard and When you do your best they say NoT Good enof

Action plans for successful learning

- Monitor the student in class. Does the student finish the seat work in reasonable time if putting reasonable effort? If not, modify the level of difficulty of the work or the volume of the work required.

- Check with parents to see if they feel that their child's workload is manageable or excessive.

- Recognize that the student may be exhausted by the end of the school day and often finds extra work really difficult to face.

- Homework for the student should be practice and review material. Keep new or demanding work for the classroom.

- Give parents constructive help in supporting the student.

  Provide an overview of the week's work ahead of time.
  Offer a "help line" to the parent.
  Authorize the parent to abbreviate, modify, and provide support with homework.
  Use a home-school communication book for exchange of information about workload.

- Set time limits on homework. The following are suggested times for student homework:

6 - 7	years of age	Maximum 15 minutes
7 - 8	years of age	Maximum 20 minutes
8 - 10	years of age	Maximum 30 minutes
10 - 12	years of age	Maximum 45 minutes
12 - 14	years of age	Maximum 75 minutes
14 - 15	years of age	Maximum 90 minutes
16	years plus	Maximum 180 minutes

- If remedial work is required, then reduce the amount of other homework.

- If classes are missed to attend remedial sessions or therapy, allow additional time for catch up work to be done, but do not exclude the student from favorite activities to do this.

- Set short tasks that can be completed in the time available, so that the student enjoys a sense of completion and develops good work habits.

- Prioritize the work required so that the least important tasks are left until last and may be omitted if time is short.

- If the student falls behind with assignments that must be completed, allow some study time during the school day to catch up, but do not exclude the student from favorite activities to do this.

- Coordinate with other adults so that the student's total work load is integrated and manageable.

- Allow the student to take short cuts. There are many suggestions throughout this book of how to do this.

- Older students may take fewer subjects to make room for extra study time.

- Make sure that the student's day is not "all work and no play".

MOTIVATION, CONFIDENCE, AND STRESS

Students with learning disabilities often have to go to school day after day experiencing failure while others are achieving success.

Some students become anxious about not being able to cope with requirements. They may fear failure and may limit their efforts in an attempt to avoid failing. While it is important to maintain a student's confidence, it is equally important to improve skill levels so that confidence is built on a solid foundation.

Students can become very disheartened and depressed by their ongoing difficulties and poor learning outcomes. This may be compounded by the physical and mental fatigue which results from the student's difficulties with learning.

Some students manage to maintain a good attitude at school but are tired, cranky, and emotional at home. Most parents give excellent practical and emotional support, although some can inadvertently put the student under additional pressure.

Action plans for successful learning

- Focus on building up skills as an essential part of building up confidence.

- All students are more interested and motivated when they can see the purpose in the task that they are doing.

- Always emphasize effort rather than outcome. A student can always succeed at putting in effort.

- Recognize that motivation comes from expectation of success. Students who expect failure do not feel motivated.

- Make praise moderately easy to get. Praise given too easily loses its value.

- Keep praise honest; children see through false praise.

Adult: *"Hey Jack, that's a great GOOD READER badge you've got there."*

Jack: *"Yeah, all us dumb readers get them."*

- Set up learning goals that are realistic.

- Make goals explicit so that everyone knows the expected outcome. For example, "Cassie will be able to read these five sight words instead of Cassie will improve her reading."

- Give a time frame for the goal. "Cassie will be able to read these five sight words by next Thursday."

- Encourage students to participate in planning their own short-term learning goals.

- Encourage students to decide what level of challenge they would like to achieve.

Let's look at the words for next week. See how you are this far along…and this is what we've got left. Now shall we go for all six words, or shall we make it three words this week and three words next week?

- Make progress visible to the student by means of record-keeping and progress charts.

- Encourage the students to mark their own progress on the charts.

- Make sure that the students can see that they are learning a lot and do not feel that they have lots to learn.

- Build in frequent tangible rewards (certificates, badges, trophies) for goal achievements.

- Provide a scope for errors on the way to success.

   Susan's goal is to be able to read the 50 most commonly used words.

   25 correct: Bronze Award
   40 correct: Silver Award
   50 correct: Gold Award

- Emphasize personal best achievements and celebrate these.

- Remember that the advice "Could do better!" or "More effort required!" is very discouraging if the students have tried their best.

- If a student is a perfectionist who won't take risks, set up a paradoxical situation and show them how to avoid failure by taking a risk.

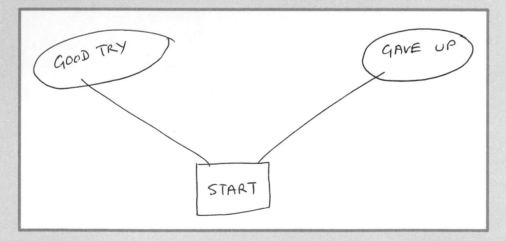

Place counters on the start position. Each time a task is presented, the student has to move a counter to GOOD TRY or GAVE UP. If there are more counters on GOOD TRY by the end of the session the student wins. Perfectionists hate to lose!

- Do not make success a burden.

> Well done, Now you have proved to me that you can do good work I will not accept second best from you in the future Jack

Jack had spent many hours on this piece of work to reach the standard that had pleased his teacher.

- Encourage self-evaluation. *What do you like best in this piece of work? If you were to do it over, what would you do differently? Are there any parts where you could have done with some help?*

- Remember that asking for help is often difficult.

  The student might think that they are doing the work correctly.
  The student may know he is confused but does not know the right question to ask.
  The student may have been reprimanded in the past for asking for help.
  The student may feel embarrassed to ask for help.

- Encourage and reward problem-solving and risk-taking. Give stamps, stickers, or tickets that can be traded for rewards.

  "You looked for another way to do it."
  "You asked for help."
  "You did not give up."
  "You had kept going until you got it."

- Make the praise specific and linked to something which the student has actually done. "I'm so proud of you; look how you remembered how write that 'b' in the correct way."

- Avoid giving negatives with positives. Try to keep praise constructive, factual, and untainted by negatives. "A good idea but spoiled by messy handwriting" is disheartening.

- Use multiple grading so that students receive feedback for content, effort, neatness, spelling, creativity, etc., as separate categories. Poor performance in one category should not wipe out a good performance in another.

- Recognize poor motivation as a signal that the student may be feeling depressed.

- Seek appropriate medical advice if the student appears to be significantly anxious or depressed.

- Make sure the student's program is modified so the student is able to see there is good chance of being successful.

- Provide counseling support.

- Provide a mentor in school to help the student to negotiate appropriate support.

- Ask parents about their view of their child's levels of anxiety or confidence.

- Make sure that parents have support and are constructively advised about their role in helping the child.

- Deal with parental anxiety by appropriate support for student and family. (See pages 103.)

- Give awards for effort and personal best achievements as well as academic and sporting excellence.

- Recognize personal qualities such as persistence, fairness, and kindness as well as academic and sporting excellence.

- Do not insist that the student read out loud in class or write on the board in front of other students.

- Keep test results confidential between student, teacher, and parent.

- Provide open-ended or multi-level tasks so that all students can work at their own level without feeling different.

- Provide the students with alternatives so that they can choose an option that suits them best.

ACCEPTANCE

It is, of course, only natural to dislike being seen as different or inferior to others. Although students may well need help, they are often reluctant to ask for or accept it. Intellectually, they may well be equal to or brighter than most of their peers, and yet they may feel stupid or dumb. Asking for and accepting help may confirm this inaccurate self-judgement in the student's mind.

Action plans for successful learning

- Where possible, find good role models of older students or adults who have had dyslexia or learning disabilities but have succeeded despite this.

- Make sure the school classroom environment is a positive one where students respect and support each other.

- Provide the students with a card which summarizes their needs. This can be shown to new teachers to clarify what type of support is appropriate.

- Create a school climate where receiving help is an accepted part of the learning process.

- Be discreet and sensitive about modifying work and giving extra assistance.

- Allow the individual students to show their talents, so that they are "different" in a positive way.

- Have a clear anti-discrimination and anti-harassment policy within school and in your classroom, where all students know the correct procedures to adopt if discrimination or harassment occurs.

- Include the students in all discussions and allow the students to give input and be part of decisions that are made about managing their disability.

- Some students have issues with regards to equity. "It's not fair that I get more time just because I have dyslexia." Explain that the intellectual content of the work is what matters and that the time allocation can easily be varied to suit individual needs. "If the test had been about how quickly you could write, then it would not be fair to give you extra time...but this project is not a speed trial...the project is to test your ideas and understanding so the time you take is not an issue."

- Ensure that the student knows that hundreds of students with dyslexia take college entrance examinations with the support of special provisions and achieve considerable success.

Chapter 9

PARENTS, PROFESSIONALS, AND SUPPORT STAFF

PARENTS

ALTERNATIVE OR NEW TREATMENTS FOR DYSLEXIA

PARAPROFESSIONALS AND VOLUNTEERS

PARENTS

Having a child with dyslexia can mean additional anxiety and stress for parents. While many parents are concerned about appearing to be fussy and over-anxious, they do carry the major responsibility for ensuring that their children have the best opportunities to reach their full potential.

Parents worry about both the practical and the emotional components of a learning disorder.

From a practical point of view, parents worry about their child falling behind other students of similar age and intelligence. Parents fear that this may mean that their child is not ready to move to the next grade level.

Parents worry that intellectually capable students may fail important subjects because of difficulties in reading, written language, or math. This could easily result in the student leaving school without graduating, even though the student is highly intelligent. Naturally, parents will feel immense anxiety if they can see that this is a possibility.

Parents also worry that their adolescent may not pursue a post-secondary education because of the disability. Employment difficulties can also be anticipated. There are, of course, many things that can be done to minimize disadvantages such as these, provided the student is recognized and given appropriate intervention and adjustments and accommodations. However, parents may not be aware of what can be done.

Parents may have additional financial costs for private assessments, remedial help, or computer resources to support their child. Since dyslexia runs in families, some parents may have to meet these financial commitments for several children over many years.

Where there is a family pattern of a learning disorder and/or an ongoing adult with dyslexic problems, parents often worry that history is repeating itself in the next generation.

Parents often comment on the fact that their child is distressed and frustrated because of learning difficulties. Many children put a brave face on things at school in front of their peers, but are tired, cranky, and distressed at home.

Parents also see their child losing confidence and possibly becoming depressed. This may be a familiar pattern repeating itself from the parent's own childhood. Parents, of course, also become concerned when the child suffers social consequences such as being teased and feeling insecure because of the learning disorder.

Parents often comment that the way which professionals handle their child makes a very important difference.

Parents report major concern when professionals do not seem to have sufficient information about dyslexia to make informed judgments or when professionals deny that the child has a problem and claim "It will click." This is a particular problem for families where adult members have enduring and severe learning disorders.

Many parents report anxiety and frustration in situations where professionals do not communicate effectively with one another, so that parents find things which had been agreed on one year are totally unknown to the next year's teacher.

Teachers and parents alike express concern when there is intermittent or inadequate staffing or funding for appropriate remedial programs.

Poor communication between school and home is another source of parental anxiety. Parents may feel that they are not informed about their child's program or progress. This is a particular problem if parents do not understand the jargon or the methods used.

Parents also worry if they believe that inappropriate expectations are being made of the child, leading to considerable frustration. For example, homework assignments for the child with learning disorders may take many hours to complete. Parents may have to devote a considerable amount of time assisting their child and the child may be reluctant and uncooperative.

In the absence of appropriate professional support from school, many parents institute their own home-based or private remedial program. The quality and effectiveness of this type of intervention can vary from exceptionally good to disastrous.

Action plans for successful working with parents

- Recognize that it is an essential parental duty to be watchful for the child's interests and to be concerned and act when problems are suspected.

- Remember that concerned parents may have very powerful personal experiences of dyslexia and its impact on their own childhood or adult life.

- Acknowledge that the child has a learning disability and is not lazy.

- Avoid giving unsubstantiated reassurance such as "It will click." or "He's a boy."

- Arrange for a comprehensive special education assessment if it has not already been done.

- Advocate for an appropriate intervention program, classroom support system, and learning program for the student. (The three have been combined as in this case the parent can only advocate for their child and provide input into the program.)

- Where school resources are limited, avoid making judgments about what the parents can afford or will be prepared to do themselves. Let them know the problem and the options, and let them make the decision about what to do.

- Set achievable goals which are specific and time-related if the student does not have an Individualized Education Plan. "Increase the number of sight words which James can read from thirty words to forty five. This goal will be achieved by October 31st." This gives the parents and student the reassurance of knowing that progress is planned and can be measured unambiguously.

- Arrange for regular updates of the student's progress.

- Determine specific goals with the student, parents, and professionals so that everyone knows what is happening.

- Be particularly aware of the pressure that homework may put on a family. Negotiate with parents and students to keep the homework at a reasonable level.

- Use appropriate adjustments and accommodations such as allowing the student to work orally or providing a reader in tests and examinations. If the student has an IEP, be sure the accommodations are listed.

- Modify school tasks and homework, such as providing shorter tasks, allowing an adult or peer to write for the student, etc. If the student has an IEP, these should be listed on the plan.

- Demonstrate good teamwork so that parents know there is communication between teachers.

- Foster frequent and honest communication between home and school, so that the parents know what is happening with the student's learning program.

- Provide practical support and encouragement so that parents can actively participate in their student's program and have an agreed role in the overall plan.

- Maintain good communication between teachers working with the student, particularly between one year and the next.

- Be sure that special provisions are made and let the parents know what is being done.

ALTERNATIVE OR NEW TREATMENTS FOR DYSLEXIA

It is important that parents and professionals are aware that there are many unscrupulous persons and organizations promoting "cures" for dyslexia. Over the years, responsible research has continually demonstrated that there are no alternatives other than quality services provided by appropriately trained, conventional professionals (teachers, speech pathologists, etc).

All known effective treatments rely on instructional methods, which are based on explicit instruction in the skills of reading, written language, or arithmetic. The evidence for the effectiveness of alternative programs which emphasize diet, exercise, or other therapies is very scant indeed.

Parents are, of course, anxious to try any new "cure" which claims success. It is often very difficult for parents to sort out the charlatans from the genuine professionals, and great caution is often needed.

Action plans for alternative or new "treatment" programs for dyslexia

- Be very wary of organizations that give themselves grand sounding titles such as "international" or other titles which, on inspection, do not relate to any officially recognized international authority or organization.

- Ask for additional information. *Could you give me copies of journal articles relating to this treatment? I am only interested in articles which have been published in reputable journals.*

- Be cautious in trusting any promotional material written to look like a genuine scientific document. Unscrupulous operators can sometimes produce a very glossy looking "scientific article" that is just advertising. When in doubt, check with someone who has scientific training such as a doctor or psychologist. Consider the following questions:

Could you give me the name of a professional teacher or doctor who could vouch for your treatment?

Would you tell me how you are going to monitor my child's progress?

How will you know when your treatment has been effective?

How will I know if the treatment has been effective?

Is it acceptable to you if I ask my child's teacher (psychologist, pediatrician) to evaluate my child before we start treatment and then after you have finished?

If the treatment does not work is there a "money back guarantee"?

What are your professional credentials? Could I see copies of the documentation of your qualifications and registration?

I know all professionals have Indemnity Insurance. Could I please see a copy of your Indemnity Insurance?

What are the side effects of your treatment? Could you please show me results of clinical studies to show that your procedure is absolutely safe?

If we start treatment and I find it is not suiting my child, am I able to stop treatment without further cost to myself?

Can you put me in touch with other people who have used your treatment who would be able to recommend you?

Could you explain to me what your treatment does, and how it works?

Could you explain to me what the limits of your treatment are? What symptoms or difficulties will it not treat?

Can you provide written information? I would like to be able to discuss your proposed treatment with our doctor (or psychologist, teacher, etc.)

PARAPROFESSIONALS AND VOLUNTEERS

Paraprofessionals and volunteers are widely used in the support of students with disabilities. Paraprofessionals are employed by the school district. Depending upon the individual district, the qualifications of the paraprofessional will vary. Some districts may require paraprofessionals to have only a high school diploma, whereas other districts may require 2 years of post-secondary education.

Volunteers may range from highly qualified people such as retired teachers to unqualified people who simply want to help.

Educators who utilize the support of paraprofessionals need to recognize both the advantages and the restrictions involved in the use of paraprofessionals and volunteers in providing services to students with disabilities.

Action plans for working with paraprofessionals and volunteers

- Paraprofessionals must be trained and supervised by appropriate qualified professionals. Paraprofessionals are not allowed to teach a new skill but may re-teach and review material with the student.

- Professionals should themselves have appropriate training in the management and utilization of paraprofessionals in the capacity of service providers for students.

- Ongoing appropriate professional development programs must be made available for paraprofessionals working with students.

- Paraprofessionals and volunteers should always work under the direct supervision of an appropriately qualified teacher or therapist.

- Volunteers or paraprofessionals should not be given responsibilities beyond the scope of their expertise.

- Volunteers should be used in a supplementary capacity, supporting the efforts of the professionals and paraprofessionals working with the student.

- At no time should paraprofessionals or volunteers be responsible for planning an individual student's program, monitoring progress, or reporting to parents or other professionals.

- Volunteers need appropriate training and preparation before they start to work with any student.

- Volunteers need to be accountable to the supervising professional, and good documentation is essential to ensure that all parties know the limits of their responsibilities.

- When a paraprofessional is used, it is important that the parents know that the student is receiving support from a paraprofessional who is accountable to a fully qualified professional.

- When a volunteer is used, it is vital that the parents of the student receiving their services know that the student is receiving support from somebody acting in a voluntary capacity.

- Celebrate, nurture, and appreciate the paraprofessionals and volunteers. They are an essential part of successful learning for all students.

Appendix

THE DYSLEXIA CHECKLIST

WORD LIST: 100 MOST COMMONLY USED WORDS

PROFESSIONALS AND DYSLEXIA

REFERENCES

THE DYSLEXIA CHECKLIST

Directions: Each item that applies to the child or adolescent should be checked off. Even items that only apply occasionally or to a mild degree should be recorded. The more items which apply to a child or adolescent, the more likely it is that the person is dyslexic or has a learning disability. However, it is important to remember that several other conditions have similar characteristics and specialist assessment is necessary for formal diagnosis.

STUDENT DETAILS

Student's Name _____ Date _____

Name of person completing checklist _____

UNDERACHIEVEMENT

- ☐ Difficulties in learning to read, spell, or write
- ☐ School work does not reflect their true ability
- ☐ School reports often say "Could do better"
- ☐ Results not reflective of the effort
- ☐ Teaching and review activities only produce small improvements

DIFFICULTIES IN COMBINING SPOKEN AND WRITTEN LANGUAGE

- ☐ Slow to learn the link between sounds and letters
- ☐ Can spell a word verbally but cannot write it
- ☐ Difficulty putting thoughts on paper
- ☐ Written language has words missing (or extra words)
- ☐ Inserts words that are not there
- ☐ Reading lacks fluency and speed

MEMORY DIFFICULTIES

- ☐ Difficulties in remembering instructions
- ☐ Difficulties in learning basics (letters and their sounds)
- ☐ Difficulties remembering words from one page to the next
- ☐ Problems learning unrelated sequences (for example, multiplication tables)
- ☐ Can learn spelling words for a test but forgets the words very rapidly
- ☐ Gets the sequence of letters or numbers wrong (for example, 13 for 31, 'on' for 'no')
- ☐ Difficulties with arithmetic; uses fingers to count
- ☐ Copies material incorrectly
- ☐ Makes the same error over and over again (for example, 'whent')

SPEECH, PHONOLOGICAL, AND LANGUAGE DIFFICULTIES

- ☐ Problems with word-finding when speaking
- ☐ Problems pronouncing long words (for example, "hostipal")
- ☐ Problems breaking words into sounds
- ☐ Difficulties in blending sounds together
- ☐ Difficulties in recognizing or producing rhymes
- ☐ Difficulties in learning phonics
- ☐ Later than average in learning to talk
- ☐ History of early ear infections
- ☐ Written language poorly structured

VISUAL MOTOR DIFFICULTIES

- ☐ Slow to learn how to write
- ☐ Poor class work (untidy, slow, messy)
- ☐ Mixes upper and lower case letters
- ☐ Difficulties in working as fast as other students
- ☐ Poor coordination; clumsy
- ☐ Loses place when reading; uses finger to keep track
- ☐ Letter and number reversals after the age of seven
- ☐ Disliked puzzles and drawing as a younger child
- ☐ Difficulties with sustained writing; hand gets tired very quickly
- ☐ Poor posture; slumps on desk when working; fidgets sitting on the floor

CONCENTRATION DIFFICULTIES

- ☐ Inattentive; in a daydream
- ☐ Easily distracted
- ☐ Diagnosed as having Attention Deficit Disorder
- ☐ Often restless and fidgety
- ☐ Often impulsive; does not stop and think; calls out in class
- ☐ Makes many careless errors
- ☐ Cannot read for more than a short period of time
- ☐ Poor organization; often forgets books, or class materials

SOCIAL AND EMOTIONAL DIFFICULTIES

- ☐ Low self esteem with regards to schoolwork
- ☐ Avoids learning tasks; "loses" books; wastes time; "forgets" homework
- ☐ Does not expect to succeed so does not try
- ☐ Gets frustrated and upset when effort does not produce good results
- ☐ Reluctant to accept help; does not like to be different
- ☐ Told to "try harder" even when working very hard

FAMILY HISTORY

- ☐ Other family members have dyslexia or similar learning difficulties.

WORD LIST: The most commonly used 100 words

These words are the most commonly used words and are the core for good reading and spelling.

Remember that reading always precedes spelling, so never teach a child to spell a word unless the child can already read it. You will find ideas for teaching reading and spelling throughout this book.

Set 1

a	in	he	am	the
big	will	come	mother	said

Set 2

it	I	is	go	me
car	and	father	look	home

Set 3

like	get	have	can	do
boy	to	see	good	you

Set 4

no	here	girl	all	up
at	that	one	this	she

Set 5

of	was	we	jump	are
play	down	my	live	thing

Set 6

when	new	did	name	yes
run	with	don't	what	little

Set 7

take	put	him	on	some
his	went	into	not	has

Set 8

two	know	can't	her	brother
over	three	sister	them	make

Set 9

away	for	walk	they	way
going	where	give	very	got

Set 10

bring	fall	too	by	let
be	fast	want	only	made

PROFESSIONALS

There are a range of professionals and organizations with varying specific expertise with regards to dyslexia and associated learning disorders. Parents and professionals should be aware of the need for a multi-disciplinary approach to dyslexia. In brief, the following professionals are frequently involved in the management of dyslexia.

School Administration

All students with dyslexia need special consideration in their educational programs. The majority of students with dyslexia with receive special education service under the umbrella of learning disabilities. The quality of the classroom and special education support varies depending upon the needs of the student and the way in which the Individual Education Plan is developed. The school administrator or administrative designee will attend the IEP meetings and signs the IEP, which is a legally binding document.

General Education Teachers

The general education teacher is often the first professional to become aware of a student's particular difficulties. Once these are noted, the general education teacher usually initiates a meeting to discuss their concerns with the parents. If appropriate the general education teacher (often in conjunction with the parent) will initiate a referral to the special education department. During this time period, the general education teacher's approach is vital in maintaining the student's confidence and motivation.

If a student does not qualify for special education services, the general education teacher is responsible for the day-to-day programming for the student. If a student qualifies for service, the special and general education teachers will plan together to determine the most appropriate program. It is very important that the appropriate accommodations are provided within the classroom. If the student meets the guidelines for special education services, the accommodations will be listed in the student's Individual Education Plan. The IEP is a legally binding document which must be adhered to.

Appropriate adjustments, accommodations, and teaching strategies have been detailed in other sections of this book. However, in brief, the classroom teacher needs to make sure that the student has a fair chance of completing work in a reasonable time frame, and with a reasonable degree of success. This may mean providing supplementary materials such as printed handouts, rather than having the student copy from the board. It may include using modified materials such as an individualized spelling list. It may involve providing additional support such as a reading buddy.

The classroom teacher will also carry considerable responsibility for supporting the student's self esteem and confidence and monitoring the student's academic, social, and emotional well being.

Special Education Teachers

Special education teachers have particular training and expertise in the management of learning disorders and are likely to work with a student one-to-one or in a small-group situation. The special education teacher will be responsible for planning and implementing the student's remedial program. The general and special educators will work together to determine how to best modify and adapt the classroom curriculum for the student to achieve success.

Specialists also have expertise in programs which have been specifically designed for dyslexic students. There are a range of published programs such as the Orton-Gillingham, Hickey, and others. Generally speaking, programs for dyslexic students follow a highly structured phonic framework.

Any program, however sound, is only a working tool and is most effective when used by a skilled teacher who can vary, modify, or select what to teach to match an individual student's needs.

The special education teacher will monitor progress and should be in a position to adjust the student's program as progress is made.

The special education teacher will often act as a liaison with other professionals and with parents to ensure that all the work being done is coordinated and well balanced.

Psychologists

Educational or developmental psychologists are specialists with expertise in assessing children's learning. Their input is essential in making a differential diagnosis of a student's learning difficulties. The psychological assessment should indicate whether the student does have dyslexia or has one of the other disorders such as a learning disability, language disorder, general developmental delay, or other learning or developmental problems. This is an essential first step to make sure that the student has dyslexia and not some other similar disorder which may need a different type of approach.

Psychologists also provide ongoing support and monitoring. Psychologists can monitor the overall progress of the student, not only from an academic point of view, but also from the point of view of emotional adjustment and coping strategies. Many students become anxious, disheartened, or lose motivation. The psychologist will have a role to play in providing counseling and advice to students, parents, and teachers.

Psychologists will also be able to provide assessment and advice, with regards to concentration difficulties, including Attention Deficit Disorder. Their input may be required in planning an appropriate management program for an inattentive or impulsive student.

Psychologists will also be important in documenting the student's learning disorder for the purpose of verifying the student's eligibility for special programs, special concessionary arrangements for assessment, and general legal protection.

Speech Pathologists

Speech pathologists have a specialist role to play in the provision of appropriate services for students with dyslexia. Speech pathologists are involved in working on phonological awareness and other language related skills. Many children have some subtle language difficulties, and most have distinct phonological problems.

A speech pathologist will often be an intrinsic part of the overall program for a student, working with the phonological and language related skills.

Occupational Therapists

Occupational therapists are likely to be involved with a student who has problems with visual motor skills, general coordination, and balance. Students who have specific handwriting disorders will often be appropriately seen by an occupational therapist, who will institute a program of treatment for the problems involved in the physical production of written language.

Pediatricians

A pediatrician may be involved in monitoring and supporting a child's development. The doctor may be one of the first to recognize a disorder emerging in the preschooler or young school child.

A pediatrician is also of vital importance in diagnosing concurrent problems such as epilepsy and Attention Deficit Disorder. The child's doctor may also be involved in diagnosis and treatment of emotional or behavioral problems associated with a learning disorder.

Child Psychiatrists

A child psychiatrist will be involved in working with a child or adolescent, where emotional or behavioral consequences follow the learning disorder. A psychiatrist can provide ongoing counseling, support, and, if necessary, medication. It may also be the case that the student has additional developmental problems, which require the specialist care of a child psychiatrist.

Counselors

Many schools have student counselors and, of course, there are counselors in community service and in private practice.

Counselors can support families and their children or adolescents who have dyslexia. They will provide general advice with regards to parenting, management, and coping strategies. They may provide individual counseling for a student with regards to practical coping mechanisms and stress management.

Support Organizations

There are support organizations for people with dyslexia, for their families, and for professionals who work with the students. The organizations may organize conferences, publish professional journals, and facilitate the exchange and sharing of information. Some organizations have special-interest libraries, resource collections, or book shops. Professionals and parents may run training programs and offer accreditation to teachers or schools that meet acceptable standards. Some organizations run a referral service to help parents or adult dyslexics find reputable service providers.

REFERENCES

Abidin, R.R. (1995). *Parenting stress index (3rd ed.)* Odessa, FL: Psychological Assessment Resources

Adams, M.J. (1990). Word recognition: The Interface of Educational Policies and Scientific Research. *Reading and Writing: An Interdisciplinary Journal* 5, 113-139

American Psychiatric Association. (1994). *Diagnostic and statistical manual of mental disorders* (4th Edition).Washington, DC

Block, C.C., Pressley, M., (2002). *Comprehension instruction: research based best practices.* New York: Guilford Press

Broomfield, H., Combley, M. (1997). *Overcoming dyslexia: A practical handbook for the classroom.* London: Whurr Publishers

Brown, G.D.A., Ellis, N.C., (Eds) (1994). *Handbook of spelling: theory, process and intervention* Chichester: Wiley

Dyson, L.L. (1996). The Experiences of Families of children with learning disabilities: parental stress, family functioning, and sibling self-concept. *Journal of Learning Disabilities*, 29, 280-286

Elbro, C., Borstrom, I., Peterson, D.K. (1998). Predicting dyslexia from Kindergarten. The importance of distinctness of phonological representations of lexical items. *Reading Research Quarterly*, 33, 36-60

Felton, R.H. (1993). Effects of instruction on the decoding skills of children with phonological processing problems. *Journal of Learning Disabilities* 26(9), 583-89

Fisher, P. (1999). Getting up to speed. *Perspectives* 25(2):12-13

Foorman, B.R., Francis, D.J., Winidates, D.et al (1997). Early interventions for children with reading disabilities, *Scientific Studies in Reading* 1:255-276

Foorman,B.R., Francis, D.J.,Fletcher,J.M., et al (1998). The role of instruction in learning to read: Preventing reading failure in at risk children. *Journal of Educational Psychology, 90* .37-55

Fuller, G.B., & Rankin, R.E. (1994). Differences in levels of parental stress among mothers of learning disabled, emotionally impaired, and regular school children. *Perceptual and Motor Skills*, 78, 583-592.

Graham, S., Voth, V.P. (1990). Spelling instruction: Making modifications for students with learning disabilities.*Academic Therapy* 4:447-457

Grigorenko, E.L. (2001). Developmental dyslexia: An update and genes, brains and environments. *Journal of Child Psychology and Psychiatry.* 42, 91-125

Henry, M.K. (1997). The decoding/spelling continuum. *Dyslexia: An International Journal of research and Practice* 3(3), 178-89

Latson, S.R. (1987). Preventing parent burnout: Model for teaching effective coping strategies to parents of children with learning disabilities. Reprinted in *Learning Disabilities Association, LDA Newsbriefs Jan/Feb*, 1995 (reprinted from the 1987 issues of LDA Newsbriefs).

Lovett, M., Borden.,S., DeLuca, T., Lacerenza,L., Benson, N & Brackstone (1995). Treating the core deficits of developmental dyslexia: evidence of transfer of learning following strategy and phonologically based reading training programs. *Developmental Psychology* 30, 805-822

Lyon, G.R. (Ed.) (1994). *Frames of reference for the assessment of learning disabilities.* Baltimore, MD: Brookes Publishing

MacArthur, C.A., (1996). Using technology to enhance the writing processes of students with learning disabilities.*Journal of Learning Disabilities* 29:344-354

McArthur, G.M., Bishop, D.V.M. (2001). Auditory perceptual processing in people with reading and oral language impairments. Current issues and recommendations. *Dyslexia,* 7 150-170

Morrison, G.M., & Cosden, M.A. (1997). Risk, resilience, and adjustment of individuals with learning disabilities. *Learning Disability Quarterly*, 20, 43-60.

Muter, V., Snowling, M., (1997). Grammar and phonology predict spelling in middle childhood. *Reading and Writing 9,* 407-425

National Reading Panel (2000). *Teaching children to read: An evidence-based assessment of the scientific research literature on reading and its implications for reading instruction.* Washington DC: National Institute of Child Health and Human Development

Oakland, T., Black J. L., Stanford, G., Nussbaum, N.L., Balise.R. (1998). An evaluation of the dyslexia training program: A multisensory method for promoting reading in students with reading disabilities .*Journal of learning Disabilities* 31:140-147

Pinnell, G.S., De Ford, D., Lyons, C., (1988). *Reading recovery: Early intervention for at risk first graders.* Arlington, VA: Educational Research Service

Rasinski , T.(1990). Effects of repeated reading and listening while reading on reading fluency.*Journal of Educational Research* 83:147-150

Rayner, K.., Foorman, B.R., Perfetti,C.A., et al (2002). How should reading be taught? *Scientific American, 286* (3) 85-91

Resta, S.P. Eliot, J. (1994). Written expression in boys with attention deficit disorder. *Perceptual and Motor Skills 79(3) 1131-1138*

Rowe, K.J., Rowe, K.S., (1992). The relationship between inattentiveness in the classroom and reading achievement *Journal of the American Academy of Child and Adolescent Psychiatry* 31(2) 349-368

Sattler, J.M. (1992). *Assessment of children-revised and updated third edition* (3rd.ed.) San Diego: Jerome M. Sattler

Semrud-Clikeman, M., Biederman, J., Sprich-Buckminster, S et al.(1992). Comorbidity between ADHD and learning disability *Journal of the American Academy of Child and Adolescent Psychiatry* 31 439-448

Snowling, M, (1995). Phonological processing and developmental dyslexia. *Journal of Research in Reading* 18(2) 132-38

Snowling, M., Hulme, C. (1997). *Dyslexia biology cognition and intervention.* London: Whurr Publishers

Snowling, M. (2000). *Dyslexia* (2nd ed). Oxford: Blackwell

Snowling, M., Bishop, D.V.M., Stothard, S.E. (2000). Is preschool language impairment a risk factor for dyslexia in adolescence? *Journal of Child Psychology and Psychiatry, 41* 587-600

Sparrow, S.S., Balla, D.A., Cicchetti, D.V. (2000). *Comprehensive psychological and psychoeducational assessment of children and adolescents: A developmental approach.* Boston, MA : Allyn & Bacon

Stackhouse, J. (2000). Barriers to literacy development in children with speech and language difficulties. In D.V.M Bishop &L.B Leonard (Eds), *Speech and language impairments in children: Causes, characteristics and outcomes.* Philadelphia Psychology Press Ltd

Torgensen , J.K.., Wagner, R.K., Raschotte, C.A. (1997). Prevention and remediation of severe reading disabilities: Keeping the end in mind. *Scientific Studies in Reading* 1(3), 2117-34

Turner, M. (1997). *The psychological assessment of dyslexia.* London: Whurr Publishers World Health Organization. (2000) ICIDH-2: *International classification of functioning, disability and health* Geneva, Switzerland: Author

Wolf, M., Bowers, P., (1999). The question of naming speed deficits in developmental reading disabilities: An introduction to the double deficit hypothesis. *Journal of Educational Psychology 91,*1-24

Wright, B.A., Bowen, R.W., Zecker, S. G., (2000). Nonlinguistic perceptual deficits associated with reading and language disorders. *Current Opinions In Neurobiology. 10,* 482-486

If you have questions or would like to request a catalog or place an
order, please contact
Peytral Publications, Inc.
We will be happy to help you.

Peytral Publications, Inc.
PO Box 1162
Minnetonka, MN 55345

Toll-free orders: 1-877-PEYTRAL (877-739-8725)
Questions: 952- 949-8707
Fax: 952.906.9777
Or visit us online at:
www.peytral.com